THE LIVING SIN OF THE MULTICULTURAL CHRISTIAN

Steve Garrett

New Harbor Press

RAPID CITY, SD

Copyright © 2023 by Steve Garrett

All rights reserved. No part of this publication may be reproduced, distributed or transmitted in any form or by any means, without prior written permission.

Garrett/New Harbor Press
1601 Mt.Rushmore Rd, Ste 3288
Rapid City, SD 57701
www.newharborpress.com

The Living Sin / Steve Garrett -- 1st ed.
ISBN 978-1-63357-280-5

All bible verses quoted in this book come from the King James bible and the New American Standard bible.

Destiny finds those who listen
fate finds the rest

Marshall Masters

CONTENTS

Introduction 1
The Strange Fruit of Multiculturalism 3
Multiculturalism is the Child of Immigration 31
Historical Grievances in America 51
Multiculturalism and the Military 73
True Multicultural Nations do not Exclude 93
Multiculturalism, the Anti-thesis of Blood and Soil 113
A divided (multicultural) nation shall not stand 129
First Principles and a Return to the Center of your Culture 169
~ 2023 ~ 211

INTRODUCTION

I have undertaken this task to write a book about a subject that is controversial at best and confrontational at worst. It must be known that controversy is not my intention. My reason for writing this book is to sound the alarm and inform the Christian of the critical error in his knowledge of a world most live in today called multiculturalism. To also help him understand how he can actually end up promoting such an anti-christian aberration. For those who have eyes to see and their hearts opened wide I am prepared to take them into virgin territory to reexamine this man created sacred cow of multiculturalism accepted today by Christianity under the mission for racial biblical brotherhood. To systematically take apart piece by incorrect theological piece the perceived belief that Christians of all races can and must dwell together as brothers within common borders.

So why am I writing this book now? The reason is to let this book serve as a warning to the Christian body of not only the United States but to the world as a whole that this elite created multicultural error accepted and promoted by the modern church of today can end up being the reason for a possible delivery of a re-activated judgment by God that I believe most Christians are not prepared to receive. The message in this book is for all denominations that serve Christ. It is for all countries with a church within its borders. It is for all races and ethnicities alike that worship the Lord Jesus. I fully realize I am walking into a minefield of controversy. Its no secret to me or anyone else that most countries, governments, schools, and churches, promote this man created phenomenon called multiculturalism. But undeterred I am prepared to take a stand and deliver this message. It will be up to each individual reader to make the decision on how he feels about what he has read in this book.

Authors note to the reader: *To get the most out of this book it is important to understand that this author is writing this book from the reference point of the Caucasian Christian and his experience with and during the transformation of America from a Christian European Nation into a multicultural country. With that being said it is this same authors hope that Christians of all colors and ethnicities all over the world will find the information in this book useful as it relates to their understanding of multiculturalism and how it impacts Gods original creation of the nation state.*

THE STRANGE FRUIT OF MULTICULTURALISM

On November 5, 2009, a Major in the United States military named Nidal Hasan decided to do his best interpretation of Allahu Akbar (Allah is the Greatest) and shoot up his fellow soldiers at Fort Hood Texas. The body count was thirteen dead and forty wounded. For those who were watching, the media was abuzz with a whirlpool of whys, and how could he's, with regards to this American born Virginia Tech graduate shooter. As America's Army and the mainstream media began their frantic search for the reason why an American soldier would cause this slaughter America had already figured it out. It wasn't hard. If you live outside the mainstream politico and media you called it terrorism.

The reactions to the killing from the U.S. Gov't and the American Arab communities in America were also the usual. Our protector in chief Barak Hussein Obama's reaction was the typical candy coated, "we don't know all the answers yet and I would caution against jumping to any conclusions." Our Army's response was no better and when the full report came out was anyone really surprised? According to a *TIME* article by Mark Thompson on Jan, 20, 2010, he reported: "The U.S. Military's just released report into the Fort Hood shootings spends 86 pages detailing various slip ups by Army officers but not once mentions Major Nidal Hasan by name or even discusses whether the killings may have had anything to do the the suspects view of his Muslim faith." CAIR (Council on American-Islamic Relations) was quick to condemn the actions of Hasan but said this random act had nothing to do with the peaceful religion of Islam. Another Muslim group called "Revolution Muslim" called Hasan an officer and a gentlemen and sent him a get well soon wish.

But just one month later in December of that same year, five American Muslims traveled to Pakistan in hopes of joining the Islamic militants in that country's tribal area. Javed Islam, a regional police officer chief in Pakistan said the five young men reportedly told the Pakistani investigators that they were trying to contact terrorist linked groups and cross the border to fight the U.S. Troops in Afghanistan. But Javed Islam said the terrorist groups turned them down because they didn't have any references.

Can we blame the creation of America's culture of multiculturalism for the actions of these citizens turned traitors? It seems all over Europe they are also experiencing similar incidents with the same social experiment. Across the pond the beloved German chancellor Angela Merkel told the *BBC* on October 17, 2010, "attempts to build a multicultural society in Germany have utterly failed." Not failed mind you but UTTERLY FAILED!

But that was then and this is now. So zoom forward and the red haired German seems to have had a change of heart. *The Washington Times* on September 10, 2015 reported: **"Angela Merkel welcomes refugees to Germany despite a rising anti-immigrant movement."**

What a difference a few years makes on the world political scene I guess. Now is this just a German aberration? Not so. As reported by the *U.K. Telegraph*: Fellow French President Nicolas Sarkosy declared on February 11, 2011, that, **"Multiculturalism has failed"** during a media conference at an EU summit in Brussels. But zoom forward to November 18, 2015 and we have the media *THINKPROGRESS* reporting that France's new President Francois Hollande **promised** to honor his commitment to take in tens of thousands of refugees.

Meanwhile a short hop and a skip across the English Channel and we have British Prime Minister David Cameron on February 5, 2011, as reported by the *BBC,* telling the world, **"State Multiculturalism**

has failed." But on May 8, 2016, the *Daily Beast* reported that history has been made. London's first Muslim Mayor was elected. The pride and joy of London, Sadiq Khan wasted no time and began threatening foreign Presidential candidate Donald Trump by saying **"Let Muslims in America or they will attack America."** The religion of peace scores again!

Here at home in the States the multicultural message is about to get real personal. May 9, 2016 *Breitbart* is reporting: President Barak Obama's administration is gearing up to pull more urban poor out of the cities and forward them into middle class suburbs. As reported by the *New York Post*, Obama's Housing Secretary Julian Castro is looking to create a new program that will relocate funding for Section 8 housing to punish suburbs for being too White and too wealthy. So now we will lose the ability to choose our own neighborhoods to raise our children in the land of the free and the home of the brave. A lot of motivation for seeking success in this country I guess.

It seems from America to the Mediterranean, the same phenomenon is happening everywhere. American and European leaders are defying the wishes of their people and opening the gates to the floods of 3rd world immigrants from every corner of the earth. To what result? Just what is the goal of these leaders who continually govern against the will of their own people? There are many theories on why they do this from laying the ground work for a third world war between Christianity and Islam as outlined by Masonic leader Albert Pike, to promoting no national loyalty by the racial dilution of countries to assist in creating a global community governed by a World Entity. But the end result is never good for the host nation. One such result that has happened in the past in Eastern Europe is the event called *balkanization*. This geopolitical term describes the process of social fragmentation, or the ethnic geographical division of a region into smaller states that are hostile or non-cooperative with each other after some type of regional collapse.

So here I am sounding the alarm as so many have done in the past. From Pat Buchanan to Frosty Woolridge, the message is clear and the results have always been the same. Empty political suits filled with empty promises no matter how many surveys, protests, and complaints, they get from their constituents about immigration. And concerning the participants of the voting booth. Pat Buchanan astutely stated, "The American people do not have the political will to stand up and stop this immigrant tide that is overwhelming their country." This caused me to come to the conclusion that if I was going to leap into this volatile issue as so many have done before, I needed some other type of reason that would provide justification for this book. Being a Christian I realized I should be seeking a higher authority to validate this message. So after some late nights inspired by mugs of coffee and some serious soul searching I arrived at the only possible answer the Christian should arrive at. That this authority had to come from God Himself. So with much prayer and contemplation I began to focus on the bible book of Genesis and more specifically chapter 11. Here is where the story of "The Tower of Babel" is and it was here where I found my much needed authority for validating the reason for this book.

After considering the story of the "Tower of Babel" and applying its historical and theological meaning to the current geopolitical environment in this country and world today, I was left with the interesting yet unsettling question of: *Does God approve of the type of country America has become today*? We all know that America is a multicultural nation filled with people from all over the world en masse who speak different languages, worship different gods, and have come here with a set of foreign values acquired from their native countries of origin. The next logical question is *"Does God approve of multicultural countries*? My new found understanding of the story of Genesis 11 tells me that He does not. In the story of the Tower of Babel we know that God separated the people of the original multicultural country as described in the bible who were building a Tower to the heavens. I haven't found any evidence in the bible that tells us God changed His mind about future multicultural countries so, it was this understanding that provided the title for this book: The Living Sin of the Multicultural Christian. In this book I have set out to prove by biblical scripture, secular events, and historical evidence, that this country called America is on a collision course with the will of God Himself. That God the Father and Jesus the Son both warned the world of the dangers of the multicultural country long ago and to dismiss Gods judgment the last time man made this mistake is to now place ourselves and our country in the direct path of another judgment from God.

So let us first take a critical look at this social experiment called multiculturalism. Let's find out who's behind it, how it impacts American society, and why it isn't working for main street America.

~ Limousine Liberals and Cadillac Conservatives ~

We in America are reminded daily that "diversity is our strength" by folks I like to call the above mentioned titles. One does not have to venture into the Liberal ideological realm very far to justify that term as it applies to them, but yes, even these new so called Conservatives have jumped on the diversity bandwagon and have appointed themselves the new guards at the Palace of Multiculturalism. These powerful culture warriors of the conservative media such as Bill O'Reilly, Megyn Kelly, and Glen Beck, look down upon us with an ever watchful eye always ready to pounce on the unsuspecting American whom they judge has violated their societal rules of their cherished plantation.

There was a time when being a conservative used to mean you were a defender of America as a European Christian Nation because the language was English, the religion was Christian, the laws were based on English law, the customs and values were European, our Holidays were Christian European, and the founders of America were all from European countries. Conservatives were basically in charge of protecting and conserving the Christian European cultural values that were passed on by our parents and grand parents. The societal norms were defended and protected by racial default for the sole reason that America as a nation back then was populated mostly by the European Christian. But somewhere in the 1960's the foreigner began to be encouraged to migrate en masse to this nation.

It was during this decade that President Lyndon B. Johnson's 1965 Family Reunification Act (also known as the Hart-Celler Act) was passed which served to unite the immigrant with his separated kin and immediate relatives of U.S. Citizens and special immigrants had no restrictions. The Hart-Celler Act also abolished the quota system based on national origins that had been the American immigration policy since the 1920's and this act also officially ended the National Origins Formula. This formula was *the American system of immigration quotas between 1921 and 1965, which restricted immigration on the basis of existing proportions of the population. It aimed to reduce the over all number of unskilled immigrants, to allow families to re-unite, and to prevent immigration from changing the ethnic distribution of the population.* Get that? The President who gave us Vietnam and the 1964 Civil Rights Act, also ended the National Origins Formula which basically was put into place to keep European Christian America, well, European Christian. Basically this one President changed the very face and direction of America during his tenure in office.

During the culture war that began in the 1960's old school Conservatives were still standing up for their Christian European nation. The last of this breed were men such as James Watt, Bob Dornan, and Pat Buchanan to name a few. These three Conservative defenders took their share of social lumps when they stood up for the cultural status quo of that time. James Watt, the U.S. Secretary of the Interior, under President Ronald Reagan (1981 – 1988) was asked to resign after making what was called an offensive statement in describing an advisory panel as ideally balanced for including "a black, a woman, two Jews, and a cripple." Now in his defense Mr. Watt did not use any offensive language when referencing these people, He was only commenting on the racial, gender, and physical breakdown of a proposed balanced panel in a not too veiled sarcastic way. But thin skins and political correctness won the day and James was shown the door. Now about B-1 Bob Dornan who acquired the nickname, B1–Bob, for his unwavering support of that alpha/numerically identified plane. All knew him as a hard fighting Conservative that verbally pulled no punchlines like "don't use the word gay unless its an acronym for "Got Aids Yet?" Bob eventually lost his seat in the House in a controversial vote count to Loretta Sanchez. Then there was/is Pat Buchanan. Certainly no stranger to the culture war zone. He has had his skirmishes with probably every liberal that lives and breathes in America today but most notably with the Jewish Lobby for his criticism during the Gulf War in 1990. He waltzed into this battle with the comment "there are only two groups that are beating the drums for war in the Middle East. The Israeli Defense Ministry and its amen corner in the United States." That's all it took. Pat was attacked from all sides by the Jewish Lobby, the Media, and many others in the Jewish population. He did survive and eventually went on to run for President a couple of times despite enduring some minor Jewish protest incidents during his campaign.

But that's how it went for the old Conservative guard back then as they were one by one swallowed up in the societal avalanche of what today is called multiculturalism. The ending result of the birth of this aberration is that the White American can no longer proudly stand up for the greatness of their once European Christian Nation without being assaulted with tireless charges of racism. You see, America is not really a Christian Nation anymore according to President Barak Hussein Obama. The success from decades of relentless attacks on these three Conservatives and others like them, coupled with a "free for all" immigration policy has basically proven Obama's statement to be true in many ways.

The governments social engineering of the American Snow White has also been a raging success as many American Caucasians now frown at their own heritage. What is social engineering one might say? Why it's the social bending process that is being promoted by the elites in the media, the government, and in our schools, to cause a person to adjust their original way of thinking on racial and cultural issues. Just watch any movie or TV Show, or read any article about the many current liberal social issues affecting America today such as gay rights, immigration, women's rights, and minority rights, and you will see the spin meisters in high gear twisting a positive view of it. But on the other side of the political coin you will witness the negative spins on Conservative issues such as White People, the military, border security, and Christianity. From the forward thinking Liberal to the backward treading Conservative, to the glories of globalism, you'll be treated to a variety of media tricks all designed to assist the unsuspecting citizen to acquire a positive impression of all liberal issues and a negative opinion of all conservative issues. Hence social engineering. This mass media campaign has been very effective in advancing the thought that the concepts of America's traditional European Christian historical past has been nothing but outdated, harmful to women, theologically oppressive, socially unprogressive, and just down right racist! The main target of this campaign is the unsuspecting White youth of America as they are skillfully guided to accept the promotion of other races pride while at the same time encouraged to condemn any thoughts they might have of their own racial pride. But racial pride in one's own country is not really an outdated concept if one looks across the ponds in either direction. Can any thinking person in America say that the Japanese from Japan have no right to be proud of being Japanese? Do you think anyone would flinch upon hearing a Chinese citizen in China saying he is a proud Chinese? Can anyone tell the Arab Saudi he cannot lay racial claim on Saudi Arabia? The White gets it when it comes to celebrating the Mexican Holiday Cinco de Mayo, or Kwanza, or Hanukah. You'll find him first in line when its time to recognize and/or promote Black History Month, or officially recognize the national convention of La Raza. Funny how that works isn't it? The pale face gets the racial nation concept when it's applied to other races but begins getting mentally confused if he starts applying that same type of racial claim to his own skin. No shouts of racism about a Miss Black America but can you imagine a Miss White America? Or how about a show, The White Perspective on the News? By now its common knowledge today that whats good for the minorities of America is not good for the White majority. By now we all should understand there are two sets of racial rules in this country today.

In the ongoing quest for equalism you'll find the Limousine Liberals and those Cadillac Conservatives on the front lines promoting, or should I say enforcing their beloved egalitarian ideology on societies great unwashed. After all, is it not true that "all races are equal" they tell us as our country is being broken into by millions of illegal aliens of color fleeing their homelands in search of a better life. Now lets all avoid the historical fact that the White American is not en masse breaking down the doors to get into Mexico, China, Saudi Arabia, or Africa, in hopes of securing a better life is he? But that's not the issue is it? We are told by the Liberals and many Republicans the issue is that it's not right or fair that you Mr. American have so much and they (immigrants) have so little. The chosen motto for our handlers should be, "You have, so you owe, therefore we must take." These self appointed anointed tell us someone needs to coordinate the transfer of all your wealth to the needy and righteous. They know if left to your own selfish devices you would do the wrong thing with your money, hence the reason they must self appoint themselves to do the right thing – with your money.

Let's examine the classic liberal ideology:

Should the American minority be proud of who he is? (Yes)
Should the White American be proud of who he is? (No)
Should the American Minority feel guilty of who he is? (No)
Should the White American feel guilty of who he is? (Yes)

The Liberal mindset tells us that Whites are bad and all others are good correct? Think not? Look no further than at this educational program called the Zinn Education Project, now being promoted by the famously liberal in Hollywood called "People Speak." As reported by the *Worldnetdaily* on January 22, 2010.

> *Hollywood celebrities and education gurus have teamed together to distribute to schools across the country a dramatic new curriculum that casts American History as an epic march of victims seeking to shrug off the shackles of the warmongering, racist, capitalist, imperialist United States. The television special features performances by Matt Damon, Benjamin Bratt, Marisa Tomei, Don Cheadle, Bruce Springsteen, and others as they condemn the nation's past of oppression by the wealthy powerful imperialist and trumpet the voices of America's labor unions, minorities, and protesters of various stripes.*

Hey, isn't that why we buy movie tickets anyway? To enrich our stars in Hollywood so later they can make the time to promote educational programs that condemn the White Christian majority, insult our ancestors, and to reduce in cultural value everything connected to our country's Christian European past? A few other tiddles the Zinn Education Projec promotes are programs such as:

The Color Line: Teaching activity by Bill Bigelow. A lesson on the countless colonial laws enacted to create division and inequality based on race. This helps students understand the origins of racism in the United States and who benefits.

The People vs. Colombus, et al: Teaching activity by Bill Bigelow. Role play in the form of a trial to determine who is responsible for the death of millions of Tainos on the island of Hispaniola in the late 15th Century.

What We Want, What We Believe: Teaching with the Black Panthers' Ten Point Program: Teaching activity by Wayne Au. The author describes how he used a study of the Black Panther's Ten Point Program to help students assess issues in their own government and to develop Ten Point Programs of their own.

So what should the reaction of these terrible White Americans be? Should they just nurture the imposed ideology of self hate and hop on the liberal guilt train to nowhere and proceed to work for the rest of their lives making reparations for their imperialist ancestors supposed oppressive past? Ask the Limousine Liberal and you will get a resounding yes vote. But the Cadillac Conservatives are not usually in the camp of self hate. You'll hear them say something like "yes there is still racism in America (only white racism of course) but America has come a long way don't cha think? So in this progressive liberal quest to seed and water America's White citizens with self hate one might ask the question why this still White majority country called American continues to be overrun by people of color who will risk their lives to dwell with those same monsters? The so called evil White person might want to ask himself if he didn't create this country called America where would all these people of color migrate to? Obviously these immigrants are not satisfied with their current living arrangements in their countries of origin correct? So as the White man contemplates how racially awful he is he can take at least some kind of comfort in the thought that this country he is blamed for creating has been the destination of choice for millions of minorities all over the world for over half a century.

It was 2003 when White students at Johnson County High in Wrightsville, GA were continuing their tradition of holding a private prom separate from the regular prom as did the Juniors at the neighboring Taylor County High that year. News of these separate proms reached the factor guy Bill O'Reilly at the Fox Network. Bill reacted angrily by demanding that Georgia's governor Sonny Perdue, attend the official Taylor County prom in protest even though there was no evidence that the White kids of Taylor County hated their Black classmates. It seems that having a preference for socializing with one's own kind, in ones own time, on ones own dime, now constitutes a form of racism in Cadillac Bill's world. But would the Cadillac Conservative apply the same cultural standard to other races? Ah, it seems our cultural warrior conveniently looks the other way when the shoe is on the other races foot.

During that same year in 2003, *Washington Post* writer Michael Fletcher wrote an article describing graduation events at the University of Pennsylvania titled: Diversity or Division on Campus? "The presentation of the class of 2003 was the central event at this year's Black Senior celebration. The ceremony here, attended by almost half of the university's 140 Black graduating seniors, followed separate celebrations that also honored Asian Americans and Latino Seniors in the weeks leading up to Penn's general graduation ceremony. University officials say these racially and ethnically themed ceremonies are a way for minority students to celebrate their cultural connections. At other prestigious colleges such as Vanderbilt, Michigan State, Stanford, and Berkeley, in 2003 they were also hosting separate ceremonies for Black graduates. It seems many other schools also have special ceremonies for honoring Latino and Asian students. Across America writes Fletcher, there are Black Fraternities, Black Sororities, and racial culture centers. Black students study in separate groups, they eat at segregated dining tables, and they unwind at separate parties."

Does this mean these Black students hate their White classmates? Of course not. They simply prefer to socialize with their own. So where were our culture warriors on this one? Funny, I just cannot recall the Factors crew calling for the governors of Pennsylvania, Tennessee, Michigan, and California, to protest those graduations. So the question reasserts itself. If it's perfectly acceptable for Black, Asian, and Latino students to have separate fraternities, sororities, cultural centers, and separate graduation ceremonies all subsidized by college dollars, why is it an outrage when White High School kids in rural Georgia have their own prom, on their own time, paid for by their own parents? It seems like our culture sheriff Mr. Bill O'Reilly is enforcing his own form of selective multiculturalism on his own perceived terms.

Be it an off color statement or a simple painless public act, the Cadillac Conservatives with their Liberal comrades in tow are on the job 24/7 sifting through our daily lives in search of perceived racial violations to flash across the nations television screens for all to witness as they play judge and jury. Heart stopping violations such as Dallas Cowboy cheerleader Whitney Isleib dressing up as incarcerated rapper Lil Wayne in black face at a Halloween Costume party makes national news with the on-the-street newsman polling Americans for their take on Whitney's Halloween costume. Does it do any good to say there might be more important issues affecting America than some cheerleaders Halloween costume? But where were our enforcers of cultural correctness with regards to the serious racial murders in Knoxville, Tennessee of two White kids, Channon Christian and Chris Newsom? The media's silence was ear shattering. By now we all know it goes without saying if Channon and Chris were Black and had been murdered by Whites in the same way America would have been drowning in media coverage.

~ The natural Consequences of unnatural multiculturalism ~

So what is this multiculturalism that currently enjoys the promotion, protection, enforcement, and absolute adoration of America's elites? Why does the government and media feel it is their sacred duty to force it upon the American people? Just where did his thing come from? One sure bet is your neighbor three houses down didn't think of it. The grocer down the way didn't either. It's safe to say that main street America didn't get together one fine day for a cookout in the 1960's to discuss how they could bring the worlds various races into their neighborhoods. Nope. This thing called multiculturalism was the brainchild unearthed by people with other thoughts on their minds. Today articles abound on the glories of multiculturalism as well as the dangers of it. It is this authors guarantee that the Liberal starlets of Hollywood will not be found pushing a loaded baby stroller down Grape Street in Watts, Los Angeles, on some cool summer night while telling the locals they don't have enough White neighbors. That being said, you will also not find the Black citizens from this same Watts neighborhood filing a complaint in their local county commissioners office stating that there is not enough racial segregation in their community. I recall a situation in Tucson, AZ many years ago where Whites were starting to move into a section of town that was historically called "the Barrio" which was located just outside downtown and started renovating the historic old houses. It was traditionally a Mexican neighborhood for many years. This caused complaints from the Mexican residents telling the media "the Whites are moving in and changing the culture of our neighborhood." Ah.... just imagine if.....well you know where I'm going. No my friends, on balance, American neighborhoods left alone are fine just the way the residents who live there decided to make them. Be they Black, White, Latino, Asian, Jewish, or? It's that other crew called the elites who are just not happy with the living arrangement decisions main street Americans make on their own.

History tells us that most cultures have displayed at best ambivalence, at worst hostility towards incoming foreigners who are viewed as posing a challenge to a fixed system of ritual, folkways, and traditions of an established culture. This traditional type of protectionist thinking is normal and expected with regards to historic organic (natural) cultures. The organic culture is one that is historically comprised of a people with common blood, a common language, common customs and values, and basically a common religion. So should we respect the racial integrity of these organic cultures in the various places of the world? I think I hear a YES! Okay, next question. Should we respect that same racial integrity of a Christian European country that wishes to remain Christian and European? I think I smell confusion.

If you are displaying the emotion of confusion I will suggest to you that your governments social engineering is being challenged. It was approximately fifty years ago give or take when America walked into the direct path of the engine of multiculturalism and that engine was and still is victimhood. You see, for multiculturalism to gain a foothold in a targeted country (read European country) the original host/culture of the targeted country must be economically and culturally brought down, as the incoming competing minority culture must be economically and culturally brought up. Hence the introduction of the liberal term into the American psyche: Egalitarianism. Which means equality between all members of a social group or society. But as Dr. Paul Craig Roberts said in his article on this subject: Multicultural Speak: *"Whites lack the moral status as a victim group. Therefore when Whites are beaten down or shouted down it is seen as retribution."* Therefore it should be understood, Whites in America cannot win in this type of multicultural social arrangement because they are the host people and therefore lack the status (engine) of victimhood. The key to the success of multiculturalism is promoting to the host culture the paralyzing effect of being labeled a racist or a bigot. The predictable results of this promoted White guilt syndrome is the relentless racial and cultural dismantling of what was once that European Christian Nation called America.

So what does a nation get when its leaders have too much money and too much time on their hands? From our experience here in America, cultural and racial dilution through unchecked immigration. Be it Democrat or Republican, the historic results of each political parties approach to legal and illegal immigration has on balance been identical. The actions of America's political leaders elected by this still White majority have caused many of the paler complexions to wince in perplexity as they ponder their country's direction today. "What happened to our America?" some say as they line up in November to elect yet another incumbent. "Why is my Christmas holiday under attack every year by my fellow Americans?" they wonder. "How come there were three language interpreters at the local PTA meeting last night?" As the *whys* and *how come*s and the *it used be* mentally back the White Christian into a corner, the next thing to follow will the the raw emotion of resentment. Strange as it may seem the historically ignorant White Christian can look nowhere but inward as he contemplates what has happened to his country. As former Presidential candidate Ross Perot used to say on the campaign trail, "keep voting for the same people, you'll keep getting the same results."

History has not been kind to multicultural nations. How can one forget the international disaster of Yugoslavia and Kosovo to be more specific. It was in the 90's when the immigrating Albanians from next door Albania walked off with military assistance and the blessing of America, the historic Serbian city of Kosovo. I would not bet against these Serbians memory of them forgetting how their beloved city was stolen. The question begs for an answer. Is this multicultural country of America created by and oh so cherished by our elites also loved just as much by main street America?

In 2007 an amazing yet little talked about five year research project on diversity in America was undertaken by one Robert Putnam which put everything in perspective. http://www.city-journal.org/html/bowling-our-own-10265.html

Putnam's study revealed that:

> *Immigration and diversity not only reduces social capital between ethnic groups but also within the groups themselves. Trust, even for members of one's own race is lower, altruism and community cooperation rarer, and friendships fewer. The problem isn't ethnic conflict or troubled race relations, but withdrawal and isolation. Putnam writes, in colloquial language, people living in ethnically diverse settings appear to hunker down, that is to pull in like a turtle.*

Now how does this five year research project fly in the face of America's favorite slogan: *Diversity is our Strength*? Funny thing, Defending that slogan actually was the intended goal of Mr. Putnam's research project in the first place. In the 41 sites Putnam studied in the U.S. He found that the more ethnically diverse the neighborhood, the less residents trusted their neighbors. This proved true in communities large and small, from big cities like Los Angeles and Boston, to tiny Yakima, Washington, rural South Dakota, and in the mountains of West Virginia. In diverse San Francisco and Los Angeles about 30% of the people said they trusted their neighbors a lot. But in ethnically homogeneous communities in the Dakotas, the figure was about 70%. So how does one justify this type of social experiment when a study of this magnitude basically proved that multiculturalism is dysfunctional and even harmful to the existing culture of a country? One would think after such revealing and convincing evidence that America's self appointed anointed would just saddle up and ride out of town with their heads between their spurs. But undaunted, unconvinced, and never-the-less, you will continue to hear those Cadillac Conservatives and their Liberal counter parts still pontificating the glories of multiculturalism. It's not that these Pinocchio's don't get it. It's just that this is something they want you to have to serve their agenda. It's their religion folks and like it or not you have a reserved front row seat in their church. As many middle class Americans of every race seek the comfort of their own to live with in places like the Chinese do in Chinatown, these promoters of forced integration watch over us like vultures from their ivory towers ready to pounce on the person who has committed the slightest perceived transgression against their beloved unnatural aberrant ideology. I can make the safe observed claim that most people left alone tend to naturally separate along racial lines in many ways. Most Whites still marry Whites while Blacks do the same, etc. People of all races for the most part take racial demographics into consideration when choosing the neighborhoods they live in, the schools their kids go to, and the churches they worship in. For some bizarre reason those in the media and government either do not understand this or don't like this, and will commit an enormous amount of time and resources to squash this type of natural thinking.

But resentment is on the rise as evidenced by the phenomenon created by current Republican presidential nominee, Donald Trump. He has sailed in on a tidal wave of popular support as he has literally overwhelmed all opponents in his way including the leaders in his own party. So what is it about this guy? Well one of his main platforms is immigration and how he will build a wall and close the borders. Gosh how long do ya think the American people have been screaming at the top of their lungs for that one? What Trump has also done without even trying is shining the spotlight on all the globalist Republican wolves that are hiding in sheeps clothing. Look no further than at Fox media darling Megyn Kelly who committed unwarranted personal attacks on Trump. I myself actually thought of Ms. Kelly as a conservative until some of her recent infamous interviews. There truly was no real reason for her to attack Trump. One has to look a little deeper into these assaults from a supposed fair and unbiased media commentator to begin to understand the motives involved. Trump is an outsider. He is not a political insider that has sworn his allegiance to the uni-party of the Republicrats. Hence a target for the controlled opposition Fox media. It was former Speaker of the House Newt Gingrich who put it all in perspective in his Fox interview during the campaign. When asked why everyone seems not to like Trump including the members in his own party, Newt calmly smiled at the camera and spilled. "Trump does not belong to the secret club. He hasn't gone through the initiation." So where are the conspiracy nuts on this one?

~ But King Solomon loved many strange women ~

The resentment caused by lowering the culture of the host people in their own country only to elevate other later added cultures is dysfunctional at best and deadly at worst. What are the bible issues of multiculturalism concerning the Christian American today? Look no further than at the story of wise old king Solomon. You know. The guy with seven hundred wives and three hundred concubines, many of them foreign priestesses.

Was God Himself practicing multiculturalism when He told Solomon in 1st Kings, not to marry foreign women? Or was God saying "hey Sol, all religions are just as good as mine so go ahead and marry all those foreigners so they can help you worship their gods." Not really. In fact God was warning Solomon that if he married those foreign women they would eventually turn his heart away from Him (God) and he would end up worshiping his wives gods. The good book tells us:

The problem: 1 Kings 11:1, *King Solomon loved many strange women, together with the daughter of Pharaoh, women of the Moabites, Ammonites, Edomites, Zidonians, and Hittites.*

The warning: 1 Kings 11:2, *Of the nations concerning which the Lord said unto the children of Israel, Ye shall not go in to them,* *neither shall they come in unto you; for surely they will turn away your heart after their gods.*

The result of the problem: 1 Kings 11:4, *For it came to pass when Solomon was old, that his wives turned away his heart after other gods.*

How did God judge Solomons marital actions: 1 Kings 11:6, *Solomon did evil in the sight of the Lord.*

Did you catch the wording in 1 Kings 11:2? The Lord was also talking to the children of Israel when He warned them (including King Solomon) not to marry into those other foreign nations. This was a warning for all the Lord's people that if they married foreigners of certain tribes these same foreigners would end up turning their hearts from the true living God. There are many other stories in the bible containing this same message so can we say it's a really big deal to God to racially mix with some foreigners. In the book of Ezra, we find the same problem plaguing the children of Israel.
Ezra 10: 1,

> *Now while Ezra was praying and making confession, weeping and prostrating himself before the house of God, a very large assembly, men, women and children, gathered to him from Israel; for the people wept bitterly. 2, Shecaniah the son of Jehiel, one of the sons of Elam, said to Ezra, "We have been unfaithful to our God and have married foreign women from the peoples of the land; yet now there is hope for Israel in spite of this. 3, So now let us make a covenant with our God to put away all the wives and their children, according to the counsel of my lord and of those who tremble at the commandment of our God;* **and let it be done according to the law.**

The bible is clear. It was Gods law the children of Israel were breaking when they married foreign women. In Numbers 25, is yet another story of a naughty Israelite caught with his hand in the foreign cookie jar.

Numbers 25: 6,

> *Then behold, one of the sons of Israel came and brought to his relatives a Midianite woman, in the sight of Moses and in the sight of all the congregation of the sons of Israel, while they were weeping at the doorway of the tent of meeting, 7, When Phinehas the son of Eleazar, the son of Aaron the priest, saw it, he arose from the midst of the congregation and took a spear in his hand, 8, and he went after the man of Israel into the tent and pierced both of them through, the man of Israel and the woman, through the body.* **So the plague on the sons of Israel was checked.**

One only has to do a little research to find many other similar stories in the bible of the Israelite's going behind the foreign wood shed and arousing the anger of the Lord. What's the point? God in His infinite wisdom understands better than we will ever understand that when you move a people of one religion next to a people of another religion a religious conflict will ALWAYS arise. So how do these stories relate to our current multicultural country we live in today? You are going to have to do a historic before and after thing to obtain the proper understanding on this one.

First, look back to a certain time when things were different in America.

Second, look at how different our current environment is now.

Finally, look somewhere in between to see what changed.

First: *Looking back we see that* – America in the 1950's was basically a bi-racial, single culture country. We were demographically speaking, about 90% European White and around 10% Black, and a smaller percentage of other races. The culture of America was European and Christianity was the country's recognized religion. From the country's founding up to the fifties the controversial issues regarding our culture were few. For those who remember, the stores were proud to put up religious Christmas displays during that holiday. Our schools proudly put on Christmas shows and only Christmas shows. Not holiday shows or multicultural holiday shows. Students and teachers alike were free from the threat of big brother to talk about religion in the schools and school prayer was in practice. Our Christian European culture was secure, unified, understood, defended, and all encompassing. We came out of World War II stronger than we went in and we were the undisputed economic leader of the world.

Second: *looking at our country today we see that* – America is a country that worships many gods. America has many races represented in large numbers. America has many languages spoken within her borders. We have civil rights laws to protect some people from others. We have affirmative action laws to give some economic priority treatment over others. We have made Voodoo worship a legal religion. We have African immigration who import the practice of female genital mutilation. Approximately six out of ten colleges and universities censor some form of speech. Mention the name Jesus in these American schools at your own peril.

Finally: *looking for changes in between these two time periods we see that* – America started becoming multicultural sometime during the sixties. It was during this time period when America's Christian European culture came under attack on multiple fronts by what was called in that day – the Counter Culture. The enemy of this new counter culture was America's morals and traditions. This assault from the Counter Culture caused America' s traditional culture to have to defend itself on three battle fronts. The first front line assault was the emerging so called Hippie Movement. The ranks of this movement were filled with the countries predominantly White youth and one of their slogans was "don't trust anyone over 30." This movement found willing allies in the new music called "Rock & Roll." This new music was steeped in revolution and with this alliance formed they both proceeded to attack traditional America on two moral targets. The first was the existing values on sexual morals; the other was on the public acceptance of illegal drug use. The second battle front was formed by the country's negro population. It was titled the Civil Rights Movement as they, led by a preacher by the name of Martin Luther King, put this country on notice that its racial status quo policies were no longer acceptable to them. The third battle front was ignited by the Women's Movement as they burned their bras and fought to get out of the house and into the workforce as equal partners of the opposite sex. After ten years of open cultural warfare with the Counter Culture, America's traditional Christian European culture was on the ropes and severely weakened on all battle fronts. It was only a matter of time before the border went wide and all who could break in did break in. Once in, illegal immigrants had Uncle Sam waiting for them with a tax break in one hand and an American job in the other. America's debt load increased as these illegal immigrants climbed over the fence and onto the backs of the American taxpayer for a ride to that destination called – on the house.

So here we are today, a multi-racial, multi-religious, multi-lingual, multicultural country whose government and media works tirelessly to destroy that last vestiges of its own historic European Christian heritage. When that cross that stood on the hill for the pride and enjoyment of all for fifty years suddenly became offensive to that one non-Christian over yonder, it is now quickly taken down and removed from the sight of all by the very judges and politicians the voting Christian majority put in office. So do we all have a little Solomon in us today? We may not all have a foreign spouse that has turned our heart towards their foreign god, but we got a country full of non-Christians tearing down our Christian religion don't we? As Solomon's wives turned him to worshiping other gods, is not America as a country today witnessing the dismantling of her Christian heritage for the reason of not offending the non-Christian/foreigner who worships a different god? While we as an individual may worship Jesus, America officially no longer worships Jesus as a country does it? After all did not our elected Muslim President Obama inform us on April 6, 2009, that America is NOT a Christian country? So what was our response? Well we elected him again for another term in 2012 didn't we.

The message is clear. As foreign women turned the heart of Solomon away from God, foreigners and non-Christians in America have turned the political heart of this nation away from its Christian God and the rest of the country is being forced to follow the turned political heart.

~ Is America still a Christian Country? ~

So is it? Do you believe you still live in a Christian country? I will make the claim that a real Christian country is one that makes no apologies about placing the Savior Jesus Christ in the unshared, unquestioned, sacred religious leadership role of a nation.

A true Christian nation can be defined as:

- A country that expects its politicians and leaders to pray in Jesus's name only.
- A country that proudly opens its government meetings with prayers to Jesus only.
- A country that's laws are based on the Ten Commandments.
- A country that opens its schools each day with prayers to Christ only.
- A country that expects its people to have reverence for all sacred Christian values.

- A country that proudly displays its Christian symbols in the prominent and even not so prominent public places for all to admire and respect.

Now lets review these same statements as it applies to America today.

- America is a country that forbids Christian prayer only by its political leaders.
- America is a country that opens its government meetings with prayers from all religions.
- America is a country that has removed a Ten Commandments display in a court house in Alabama and threw the judge out of office who put it there.
- America is a country that officially banned school prayer in 1962,
- America is a country that now officially recognizes all religious customs from all religions.
- America is a country whose government will support the non-Christian citizen when he calls for the removal from public sight symbols of Christianity.

Where will you find the voting Christian today? Why shaking his head telling us this year he will vote for the lesser of two evils. But did we actually have a choice? Pat Buchanan ran as an America first candidate with one eye on the border and the other on an immigration moratorium in 1992, 1996, and 2000. Then there have been others like Tom Tancredo and Ron Paul who also were America first Presidential candidates. Where was the Christian voter? Voting for the lesser incumbent of two evils as always. To sum it up the Christian voter who is still the majority in America has received exactly what he has voted for and that would be an anti-Christian nation.

So let's review the wonderful benefits that we have received from the multi-culture that we Christians voted for.

- The *culture of your country says*: The life of the unborn child hinges on how inconvenient it might be for the parents.
- The *culture of your country says*: Many of our schools are now violent Godless battle grounds with pregnant girls and sexual predatory teachers.
- The *culture of your country says*: Our once proud Christian religion is shunned in public for fear of offending Muslims, Jews, Pagans, and the Atheist.
- The *culture of your country says*: Our media pop culture promotes individual and family dysfunctionalism as the norm in society. It advocates materialism, glorifies killing, promotes sexual promiscuity, and encourages degradation of our countries founding religion.
- The *culture of your country says*: We have had a politician elected in Congress who after being voted in took his oath not on the bible but on the Koran.
- The *culture of your country says*: We have had a President, a self professed Christian, celebrate the Muslim holy day of Ramadan in the White House. His name is George W. Bush. Does this sound eerily similar to another leader named King Solomon?
- The *culture of your country says*: The current President of our nation Barry Sotero with his adopted Muslim name Obama, carries in his pocket a statue of the Hindu monkey god, Hanuman for luck. Is this President not practicing a form of worship to a foreign god albeit foreign to the majority of America's original religion? This same President also broke with tradition and skipped national prayer day at the White House in his first year on the job. Further, in April 2009 before speaking at the Catholic Institution at Georgetown University, the

Obama administration requested that all religious symbols and relics be covered or removed. What's surprising is the Catholic Institution did it. To add to all this anti-Christian behavior of Mr. Yes-we-can, it was reported in his first year in office that the Obama's wanted to have a non-religious Christmas holiday at the White House. In the end tradition prevailed but not in favor of the Obama's.

This is who the voting majority of Christian America chose to lead them twice and have him represent them to the world. So as the government of your country continues to attack the very name of Jesus the undeniable truth is there for all to see and that is America always gets what she votes for. Maybe it's time to ask yourself these two questions. First, what kind of a country is it that votes for a leader that celebrates an Islamic religious holiday in its most prestigious government building? Second, what kind of country is it that chooses yet another leader that carries around a Hindu monkey god charm in his pocket?

Surely, as your latest elected leader has told you. Not a Christian country.

MULTICULTURALISM IS THE CHILD OF IMMIGRATION

The culture that ended up multi usually got there by government mandated mass immigration. One almost always cannot happen without the other. Why is this? Because if it wasn't government enforced upon the people then how did it end up that way? Did the people of Tennessee ask the Arizona, Texas, and California governors to open their borders so more immigrants could come in? Not likely and not hardly. So armed with this understanding the question sure hacks into my mind and that is how can any serious thinking person believe that if you geographically ram one type of racial people into another type of racial people that some type of divisive impact will not happen? For example, say a people of an Asian culture is located in one area and then you import en masse a large population of Europeans to live with them. Can you not think that the existing Asian culture will not be damaged, diluted, or at least changed to a degree? That this change could cause the Asians to begin to feel their way of life is threatened to a point which could produce a level of conflict? It is a guarantee that the status quo of the original host culture will be altered and history tells us this will have a negative impact on them in a variety of ways. But once the sharing begins one culture has to change or you will have two side by side cultures competing for common geographical resources. During this uniting the incoming new culture usually takes the lesser role to the dominant host nation. The lesser can experience a racial/cultural resentment as they cry foul as they are to a degree forced to change in a variety of ways for the benefit of the greater. Or the host nation might cry foul if the newbies try to force any cultural changes on them. Anyway one flips it the host culture is going to experience a nation altering social, political, and economic impact, on their original culture with the arrival of the newbies. Shall we let history be the judge of these so called elites adventure into their multicultural experiment here in America?

~ For 911 press 1 for English, 2 for Spanish, 3 for.... ~

With diseases once thought conquered now on the rise in America due to un-vaccinated immigrants, to hospitals closing down in California due to being overwhelmed by un-paying illegal aliens, the impact of unchecked immigration is weighing heavily on the medical industry in this country. Couple that with a rise in the price tag of welfare for the immigrant and an increase in the criminal element and you must ask yourself the question: How long can we really afford to be so ignorant? While the immigrant march continues across the border with the usual wink and nod from the Republicrats, the thinking person often wonders just what is the benefit of mass immigration? Just what excites these politicians about unchecked immigration be it legal or non-legal? Somewhere I read or at least heard that these Senators and Representatives including our President were elected to serve their constituents. Like they have this title Public Servant because they were elected to serve the public right? Since the illegal immigrant is supposed to be barred from voting why do our politicians keep the doors of this country flung wide open for these non-voting law breakers? Mainstream America continues to concur on this issue. The people have spoken and they want illegal immigration stopped. According to a March 8, 2016, *Bloomberg* survey, the results are in, "Americans really don't like immigration. Sixty-one percent says it jeopardized the nation. The *Rasmussen Report* concurred on February 23, 2016, "Most voters continue to favor stricter border control over granting legal status to those already here illegally and believe amnesty will just encourage more illegal immigration." So what's the problem?

The problem is there is no problem. The majority of your elected officials want America to be borderless, crime ridden, disease infested, bombed by terrorists, and economically destroyed, by unchecked immigration. Rough statement? Well lets examine this author's claim shall we? If these politicians didn't want these events to take place would they not work to prevent these things from happening? Have I been misled or is it the bold truth that they have the power to close the border and deport criminals? When Rep. Tom Tancredo from Colorado was in office he put forth a plan to fix the illegal alien problem. He introduced the Mass Immigration Act, which had called for halting illegal immigration and a three year moratorium on all legal immigration to allow those immigrants already in the country to be assimilated. When last introduced in 2003, the bill had a measly 11 co-sponsors. Think this important bill got passed? Mr. Tancredo said the way to fix the illegal alien problem was to stop all economic assistance to them and fine all employers who hire them and the eventual result would be that they would have to go home because the government incentives would cease to exist. They would have no reason to stay and it wouldn't cost the U.S. Tax payer a dime. Newsflash! It would actually save the U.S. lots of money in welfare costs, medical care costs, and school funding. It would also reduce crime and throw a whole lot of jobs back at the American work force. Ah just a little too simple for our elected protectors I guess. Lets take a closer look at these five immigration issues listed. **Borders**, **Crime**, **Disease**, **Terrorism**, and the **Economy**. Let's see how our elected protectors not only let these things happen here in America but actually work to promote them.

~ Is there really such a thing as a border anymore? ~

Issue #1. **Borders.** President Ronald Reagan once said, "a country that can't control its borders isn't really a country anymore." And what did that paragon of American conservatism do to protect those borders he was jawing about? Why he granted nearly three million illegal aliens amnesty during his tenure that's what! Think about it. If the last so called great conservative President granted amnesty to millions then promptly left the borders wide open afterwards, can we say that ole Dutch was the one who built the launching pad for millions of future incoming illegal immigrants? Do we as Americans really even have a border anymore? We think we have a northern border with Canada for the sole reason that Canada is not flooding our country with needy immigrants. But one look south and things start to get fuzzy.

Look, everyone knows what a border is. Even our politicians seem to know what one is when it pertains to a foreign country like say South Korea. In fact America has maintained a military presence there for over half a century for the specific mission of.....here it comes. Protecting South Korea's border! Since the North Koreans haven't crossed the 38th parallel in all those decades can we make the assumption that our politicians and our military leaders know how to protect a country's border? Aren't we protecting real estate in Iraq and many other countries around this rock? Can we confidently make the claim that our elected officials get the border concept when it comes to protecting borders in far off lands but have not shown that same interest when it comes to protecting their own country's borders? We still have a big enough army to protect our borders don't we? This isn't a resource problem. It seems our elected heros in office see the wisdom of using the military to protect other countries borders so why is it different here at home?

Using just a few ounces of brain matter sandwiched between the two pockets of earwax in my skull bag I can surely make the claim that the results are in and our border patrol is not getting the job done. To me it is more like they are not allowed to get the job done. So why not take the next logical step that so many countries have done before and militarize our border? We already have this experience in South Korea and its working so why not practice a little bit of that success here at home?

Well I think now it's time to play that game: Who said we will not militarize our borders!

May 15, 2006,....The United States is not going to militarize our borders. (Bush Jr.) http://www.nytimes.com/2006/05/15/washington/15text-bush.html?_r=0

March 12, 2009,....I'm not interested in militarizing the border. (Obama) http://www.sandiegouniontribune.com/news/2009/mar/12/1n12border233731-obama-opposes-militarizing-border/

Can it be any clearer? Our Presidents with their comrades in Congress do not want a border at all in America because they will not obey the will of the people or follow our country's laws, or use the resources and power given to them to protect our borders. So again you must thank your politicians for a job well done and understand this. They are only doing what they want to do.

~ Does your candidate want more crime in America? ~

Issue #2. **Crime**. Most of your State and Federal politicians want crime, look the other way when they can do something about it, and actually will spend time working to increase crime in their respective districts and states. The first reaction to this statement from our pillars of virtue in office will be the hollering of the typical, "How dare you say that! Why my record on crime is second to none in my state!" It is here where I cannot even muster up enough reaction energy to yawn. It stands to reason if one wants an ice cream one goes out and buys it. If one wants a date one goes out and asks for it. If one wants crime, then he will either go out and commit it or make it easier for a criminal to come to him and give him that crime. To use an analogy: Say you have decided that you want your house robbed. At this point your actions will be that you can advertise in the local media for it, and /or put a sign in your front yard telling criminals what your have in your house to steal and when you will be gone or at least when you will be looking the other way. Sooner or later depending upon your marketing skills you'll get what you advertised for if the advertised loot is attractive enough. Following me on this concept? So to connect the dots to our elected protectors. If a politician wants criminal illegal aliens to break into his country or state he can do one of two things. A) Do what he historically has done best which is wink and nod then look the other way when illegal immigrants cross his border. Or B) This politician will pass laws that will cause the criminal to know he will have a good chance of success when making the break-in attempt and he will receive an attractive benefit when he does. I can make the claim that most politicians do both A and B. To take this a step further. Would a President, the man elected to protect his country knowingly allow criminals into his country on purpose? Sure he would if he was an American President.

On November 28, 2005, President Bush W. speaking in Tucson, conceded that in five years, 4.5 million illegal aliens had been caught attempting to break into the United States. Among that 4.5 million, Bush admitted were more than 350,000 with criminal records. That means one in every twelve illegal aliens the U.S. Border Patrol had apprehended was a criminal.

http://www.ontheissues.org/Archive/State_of_Emergency_George_W_Bush.htm

So upon revealing that info to the Arizonans did Bush immediately change his policy and build that fence to help fix the problem plaguing the citizens of America? Did he have the power to build that fence? I think we all know the answers to these two questions don't we? Well you know the drill. Zoom forward to see what our current hero in office is doing to help his citizens concerning the danger of unchecked illegal immigration.

Obama Claims Power to Make Illegal Immigrants Eligible for Social Security and Disability. CNSNews.com April 6, 2016.
Obama reinstates "catch and release" policy for illegal immigrants. The Washington Times, Feb 4, 2016.
Obama actions shield most illegal immigrants from deportation. *The Washington Times*, Nov. 19, 2015.
Border Patrol agents say agency's gun recall puts them in danger. *Fox News Channel*, Nov 12, 2014.
Obama's illegal Aliens: Importing Deadly Third World Diseases. *FrontPage Magazine*, July 23, 2015.

Lets break this down into the simplest of terms. If one does not want to do something one will not do it. These Presidents have the power to shut down the borders and illegal immigration. As Bush informed us back in 2005, one in every twelve illegal aliens were criminals. Balance that percentage in the millions today and Houston we have a problem. What has been this Presidents reaction to this problem? N-O-T-H-I-N-G!!!

So let's sew this up shall we?

1. These Presidents and Politicians were given the power by the people to enforce the laws of this nation.
2. The people want the borders shut down and illegal immigration stopped.
3. These Presidents and Politicians have the power to stop it.
4. These same have the resources to stop it.
5. They admittedly know about the crime and other negative issues associated with illegal immigrants.
6. These Presidents and Politicians don't want to shut the borders down and halt illegal immigration or they already would have.

7. Hence, they are doing what they want to do and that is cause more crime for the citizens of America.

Criminal aliens breaking into this country is no secret to your government. In Pat Buchanan's book: *State of Emergency,* He cites: A New Century Foundation study "the color of crime" that used FBI and Justice Department crime figures found that while Hispanics are three time more likely than White Americans to be convicted of serious crimes requiring incarceration, they are nineteen times more likely to belong to street gangs. In 1980 our federal and state prisons housed fewer than 9000 criminal aliens. By the end of 1999 these same prisons housed over 68,000 criminal aliens. Today criminal aliens account for over 29% of prisoners in the Federal Bureau of Prison Facilities. These illegal alien prisoners represent the fastest growing segment of the federal prison population. Are these statistics available to our elected officials or just me? Probably one of the most powerful vicious gangs from south of the border is the MS-13 gang, or Mara Salvatrucha 13. This gang first arrived in the USA by way of California in the 1980's and that state continues to have the largest concentration of members. However, recently the gang experienced a growth spurt making it the fastest growing gang in all America in both numbers and territory. Virginia, South Carolina, Maryland, and other eastern states are now experiencing the criminal impact of this gang. Do your elected heros in office care that this gang is coming across our borders to terrorize the U.S.? To be fair, they probably care about it as much as they care about the other criminals they are helping to get into this country. How do your patriotic politicians help encourage the illegal criminal element to get into your country to cause their crimes?

1. Make sure the borders are not secure.
2. Under staff and under equip our Border Patrol.
3. Guarantee jobs to illegal immigrants.

4. Give them free medical care.
5. Guarantee them welfare benefits.
6. Give free schooling to all illegal immigrants children.

Sounds to me like a whole lot of motivation for the immigrant to make the trip don't it? With the lame stream media and Hollywood looking over their shoulders, these elected defenders of the Republic have chosen their side of this issue. With a one-eyed wink and their left hand in your back pocket, the financial carrot to the illegal immigrant is just a little too lucrative to pass up.

Now stepping back and looking at illegal immigration as a whole we all know that not all illegals are of the criminal element and most I would say are just doing what is best for them and their families. We also know that not all illegal immigrants are Mexican. So with that in mind we as Americans can complain all we want but when someone we put in office on our side of the fence is continually waving a basket of goodies in the general direction of Mexico, a reasonable individual from Mexico or wherever is eventually going to make the trip to pick it up. It's true that the illegal alien just seeking a job is many times being coupled with the criminal element. But once in this illegal immigrant must operate just outside the American system fully tax exempt while using resources meant for the American citizen. Calculating their numbers in the tens of millions you can draw a picture in your mind of the financial collision we as a nation are speeding towards. As unchecked illegal immigration continues to flood the country with a criminal element piggybacking on them you must thank your local, state, and federal, politicians because after all, they are only doing what they want to do.

~ Is there a doctor in the White House? ~

Issue #3. **Disease**. Is catching diseases more likely with unchecked illegal immigration? If that migrant is coming from a 3rd world country it is. Politicians cannot be too concerned with disease in America because they work diligently to make its arrival consistent and in large doses by their support of the entry of the carrier in the form of medically unchecked illegal aliens. Now I am not saying all illegal aliens have diseases but looking backwards for 40 years only 900 cases of leprosy had been diagnosed in the U.S. But in the first three years of the 21st century, 7000 cases were discovered here. But hey, not to worry, the CDC is on the case and will have things back to normal right? I mean that's one of the reasons we pay the Center for Disease Control isn't it? A *Brietbart* article on May 17, 2016, informed the general public that 22% of resettled refugees in Minnesota tested positive for Tuberculosis. Today four states, California, New York, Texas, and Florida, have more than half the nations active TB cases, though they have only a third of the country's population. But it is these four states that have the highest concentration of foreign born residents. Again looking in Pat Buchanan's book: *State of Emergency,* he says "because many of the legal and illegal immigrants come from rural areas in impoverished nations where sanitation is poor, they impose unforeseen costs on Americans such as the re-introduction of diseases that doctors here eradicated long ago." So as World Refugee Day was celebrated this year *Breitbart* offers another article concerning the rise of returning diseases here in America. Http://www.breitbart.com/big-government/2016/06/19/diseases-thought-eradicated-world-refugee-day/

These returning diseases are:

1. Tuberculosis
2. Measles
3. Whooping Cough
4. Mumps
5. Scarlet Fever
6. Bubonic Plague

The near eradication of these diseases in the United States during the 20th century was a remarkable accomplishment of the American civilization. Until recently most Americans believed these diseases were gone from our shores for good.

Consider that it was reported by *Fox News* on March 18, 2005, that in Los Angeles, 60% of the country's uninsured patients are not U.S. Citizens. These immigrants are overcrowding emergency rooms because they cannot afford to make the traditional doctor appointment. Then Worldnetdaily reported in California between 1993 and 2003, sixty hospitals closed down because of unpaid services and another twenty four closed in 2004. http//www.wnd.com/2005/03/29329/#. Now I could go on and on with the facts, the statistics, and the stories, but why should I? It's not that hard to understand that if you give 20 million illegal immigrants free medical care sooner or later negative economic fissures will begin forming in our nations healthcare industry.

But who's the lucky one to get handed the bill for all those free services? Not your congressman servicing himself at the public trough. Don't forget it is him who is waiving the goody bag at the border for all to see. As your medical bills go through the stratosphere like an outbound rocket, always remember your congressman and senators wanted diseases and closed hospitals so that it would eventually cause a healthcare crisis in this country. Lets not forget our friend Rahm Emanuel's famous statement: "never let a good crisis go to waste." So with crisis in hand, it is the government to the rescue with a national healthcare plan that eventually became known as Obama Care. The holy grail of progressive liberalism. They did it with the ole – Action + Reaction = Forced Government Solution. Funny how that worked out wasn't it? Who would have known?

~ A little bipartisanship goes a long way ~

Issue #4. **Terrorism**. Do politicians really want us to be bombed by terrorists? Ask the guy or gal in the Senate or House and you will be entertained by their canned flag waiving response. But then again one look under the Congressional rug and you'll see what just crawled in under their watch. The 1990 U.S. Immigration Law S.358, sponsored by former Senator Ted Kennedy, (D. Mass.) instructed State and Department employees that: *"Merely advocating terrorism, or belonging to a group that engages in terrorism, cannot be used as grounds for exclusion from a U.S. Immigration visa."* The new law focused more on activity than beliefs. Only statements that directly further or abet the commission of a terrorist act may properly constitute a basis for denying a visa. In a 2005 review of this law by the *Center for Immigration Studies* by James R. Edwards Jr. titled, *Keeping Extremists out,* "the 1990 Immigration act for the most part gutted ideological exclusion and loosened the legal and procedural barriers to entry by aliens who radically oppose the United States. It embraced an extreme vision for expanding border crossing rights to America's enemies. It revised the grounds for exclusion shrinking them from 33 grounds to 9. The Act also narrowed grounds for deportation from 19 to 5." Another beer please!

Now what did that Republican President by the name of George Bush Sr. have to say about this Democratic sponsored bill after he signed it into law?

> *"Today I am pleased to sign S.358, the immigration Act of 1990. This bill is good for families and good for business. There we go, well done, Thank you."*

So eleven years later something called 911 hits us right between the eyes and finally wakes up everyone in the government right? Uh.... no. News site *Vdare* gives us the damning report:

THE LIVING SIN • 43

"*The Washington Post* September 21, 2007: Nearly 10,000 people from countries designated as sponsors of terrorism have entered the United States under an immigration diversity program with relatively few restrictions. The report by the U.S. Government Accountability Office, said the State Department's Inspector General warned in 2003 that the Diversity Visa Program posed a significant risk to national security and recommended it be closed to people from countries on the U.S. list of state terrorism sponsors."

Well that does it doesn't it. The evidence is clear. Even the Government now knows this program is dangerous and must be sunsetted to protect the American people right?

Department Notice: The 2016 Diversity Visa Program (Section 131 of the immigration Act of 1990) (DV-2016) will open at noon, Eastern Daylight Time (EDT) (GMT-4) Wednesday, October 1, 2014, and will close at noon Easter Standard Time (EST) Monday, November 3, 2014. Applicants must submit entries electronically during this registration period using the electronic DV entry form (E-DV) at dvlottery.state.gov. Paper entries will not be accepted. http//www.state.gov/r/pa/prs/ps/2014/09/232251.htm

I am so grateful our government is preserving our precious resource of trees and trying to do the right thing by going paperless.

So looking at the sponsored laws and voting records of your elected protectors it is clear they they provided welcoming flowers and a boat load of incentives for incoming immigrants who either belong to terrorist organizations or harbor terrorist ideologies against our turf. Hey, I'm just saying if you continue to let in foreigners from nations that sponsor terrorism then is it really a stretch to expect some violent undesirables will be let in? Just saying.... There seems to be a very long and consistent dangerous pattern here with the way this Hill crowd in DC operates with regards to immigration. But hey I'm a fair guy. Judge for yourself how accurate George Herbert Walker Bush's comment was in 1990 when he signed S.358 into law.

"This bill is good for families and good for business. There we go, well done, Thank you."

~ **The American Candidates slogan of the day: I'm for jobs?** ~

Issue#5. **Economy.** What to do about your economy when your country is leaking jobs like a water levy in New Orleans? Why punch some more holes in it of course or at least try and create more competition for the fewer remaining jobs left in the country by inviting the worlds immigrants to have a crack at them. So let's try and put this all together for our elected officials benefit and general enjoyment.

Say we have 100 jobs to be filled in America and we have 120 Americans who are looking for work. At this point our politicians will import 10 immigrants to compete for those same 100 jobs. Do the math.

Don't tell me your politicians don't know there is a job shortage here in America, so the next time you hear some empty suit hollering about how he's for putting people back to work, ask him which people is he talking about? Americans or illegals. Some people revert back to the worn out but still promoted phrase "the illegal immigrant only does the jobs Americans don't want to do." Is this true? Last time I checked the American citizen had no problem working in the construction industry as well as the restaurant industry. But drive by just about any construction job site and what kind of people will you see with hammer in hand? According to an article by *TRCB.com*, "Many people living in Canada and the U.S. are worried that illegal immigrants are filling job opportunities, making it difficult for legal citizens to find work. And while the construction industry grew by 5%, the number of Hispanic workers in that industry grew by 14%." According to the *Bureau of Labor Statistics* in 2014, Hispanic workers in the construction industry was 27%.

How about the unemployed youth of America today? Think they might want some of those jobs the Mexicans are taking at the local restaurants? According to an article by Peter Coy, on *Business Week/ MSNCB* on October 11, 2009, he goes on to say "Bright, eager, and unwanted. While unemployment is ravaging many parts of the global work force, the most enduring harm is being done to the young people who can't grab onto the first wrung of the career ladder. In the U.S.. the unemployment rate for 16 to 24 year olds has climbed to more than 18%, from 13% a year ago. This is the highest level of unemployed since the government began counting back in 1948." Think that's fair for America's youth to have to compete with the illegal immigrant for a job in their own country?

With all the terrible job losses in America today you would think our elected protectors would be concerned about the unemployed right? Not so says the Government Agency, H1B and Resource Center. This is the agency that provides government assistance to foreigners to relocate them here to take American jobs. So how well has our government program that you are paying for been doing?

Year:	H1B CapDate	H1B CapDate
2010 (FY 2011 cap)	85,000	January 26, 2011
2011 (FY 2012 cap)	85,000	November 22, 2011
2012 (FY 2013 cap)	85,000	June 11, 2012
2013 (FY 2014 cap)	85,000	April 5, 2013
2014 (FY 2015 cap)	85,000	April 7, 2014
2014 (FY 2015 cap)	85,000	April 7, 2015
2016 (FY 2017 cap)	85,000	still hard at work at it

Yes the flood of these "soon to be legal" immigrants taking American jobs is alive and well with the full blessing of your President and your Congress. How's that hope and change working out for ya America?

Now of course we could begin going down the line listing each industry that the immigrant is working in but I think you get the big picture here. They are here, wages are down, and jobs are getting scarce. What seems to be lost on most of these worshipers at the altar of the border-less global agenda is that here in America there was a time that its citizens did do all those jobs now being done by the immigrant. But there was one difference wasn't there? These jobs paid a living wage back then. Today the boss man looking to buy that new speed boat has an economic incentive to hire the illegal immigrant instead of the American citizen. With less pay and usually no insurance benefit plans to deal with, the temptation to replace Joe Mainstreet with an illegal alien is financially motivating.

This whole illegal immigration process has ended up being a game between three contestants and the prize for the winner of this game is divided between the boss man and the illegal immigrant. The illegal immigrant gets a better job and a boat load of other government benefits offered by the host country and the boss man gets the cheap labor and that boat. The 3rd contestant and the loser of this three way game is the citizen taxpayer. All he gets is less job opportunities and stuck with the bills that come with the immigrant. Like welfare bills, medical bills, school bills, and a little more crime thrown in for good measure. To sum up our immigration non-problem of the five issues just discussed as it relates to the thinking and actions of our elected protectors, we understand:

- Politicians understand the importance of **borders** in foreign countries and have and will commit significant resources of this country to guard those borders.
- Politicians will knowingly increase **crime** by allowing unchecked legal and illegal immigration on a massive scale to enter this country thus ensuring a percentage of a criminal element will slip through.
- Politicians not only don't mind immigrants bringing **diseases** into America but actually will provide a very lucrative incentive for the carriers of those diseases to make the trip.

THE LIVING SIN • 47

SIDE BAR: *On January 4, 2010, President Obama lifted the ban on travelers coming to America who are infected with AIDS. For the past 22 years if you had HIV or AIDS and weren't American you couldn't enter the U.S.*

- Politicians pretend to have trouble calling **terrorist** acts terrorist acts. And through laws enacted by themselves they actually work to make it easier for the terrorist to reach their targets here in the U.S.
- Politicians knowingly work hard to destroy the **economy** by exporting jobs out of the country while at the same time importing more legal and illegal aliens to take jobs in this country causing a rise in unemployment for American citizens.

So always remember, your elected politicians know that illegal immigration increases crime, promotes a national proliferation of diseases, increases the risk of terrorism, and is an economic disaster for the tax paying citizens of America. They know the American people have spoken and overwhelmingly want the borders closed. So why won't they? Simply, they don't want to because it doesn't serve their global agenda.

Does God give us any guidance with regards to the issue of borders? Surprisingly yes for some, not so surprisingly for others. The Nation States were first established by God as a judgment in Genesis 11, in the Tower of Babel story. In this story there was a man named Nimrod who attempted as some interpret it to set up some type of New World Order government by building this tower to the sky so he could actually start some type of war with God. As judgment, God scattered the people all over the earth and then changed their once single language to many, thus establishing the first separate and defined racial nations of the world. Because of this judgment, in Africa we find Africans, in Europe we find Europeans, in Asia we find, well you get the idea. So can we as Christians understand that the nation/

state was created by the will of God? That this same nation/state is defined by not only its race, its language, but by geographical borders also? God tries to lend a helping hand for those who have ears to hear.

Deuteronomy 32:8.

> *When the Most High divided to the nations their inheritance when he separated the sons of Adam, he set bounds of the people according to the number of the children of Israel.*

Now there are those who believe the Old Testament is no longer relevant and really is just for historical research so can I throw in a passage from Acts?

Acts 17:26.

> (God) *and hath make of one blood all nations of men for to dwell on all the face of the earth* **and hath determined the times before appointed and the bounds of their habitation**.

Bulls Eye! See the words "all nations" in this scripture? God is not talking about Jack and Mikes front yards. So both the old and the new testaments concur. God not only separated the worlds people into the racial nation state and changed their language but He also set the borders for their habituation. To the Christian this should be a no brainer. If God cared enough to create man as He also cared enough to create the earth for man to dwell on, is it not too far of a hop and skip to believe He would apply that same principle of caring also on where His creations would live on His planet?

The lesson here to be understood is the multiculturalist uses immigration like a pusher uses heroin. He continually injects the drug (immigration) into the victim (host nation) until the user no longer lives, or in other words, the nation/state as it was is changed to be no longer what God created it to be. That is their goal. To kill the homogeneous

God created organic nations which will enable them to birth their unnatural Godless multicultural experiment which will in their words be under their control.

HISTORICAL GRIEVANCES IN AMERICA

One of the disadvantages of having a multicultural nation is that it had to be put together unnaturally in some way and it's a good guess that at some point in time someone had to move over for someone else to move in. And sometimes that moving over can feel more like a shove. It's that shove that can cause a grievance that can acquire a history with the people impacted. And once those two elements are combined it can produce an "historical grievance" that usually never goes away. If it's a grievance of one people against another that involved a conflict at some point in time, it is usually documented by the winning side as a conquest while the losing side remembers it as an evil perpetrated by some type of foreign invader. Does America have an element of its population that just might harbor an historical grievance against her? I guess the quickest answer is yep. America is a country that has acquired three historical grievances. At the least these grievances produce a perpetual thorn in the cultural side of this nation, at worst they could end up facilitating the birth of the most dangerous 5th column. A 5th column can be a clandestine group or a faction of subversive agents who attempt to undermine the host country's solidarity by any means at their disposal. As long as the grievance has a portion of the offended population willing to keep the flames of remembrance burning it will have the continual effect of chipping away at the cultural health of the host country.

Grievance #1
~ The Indians lost the war ~

Let's begin with the first historical grievance that was lodged against America. The Indian grievance. Here is where you will find not only the Indians historical grievance but a part of the defining center of the American liberal ideology as well. After all did not the White man Columbus come to this chunk of real estate and take it away from the Indians? Here history takes many turns. On August 3, 1492, Columbus set sail from Spain to find an all-water route to Asia. More than two months later, Columbus landed on an island in the Bahamas that he called San Salvador; the natives called it Guanahani. For nearly five months, Columbus explored the Caribbean, particularly the islands of Juana (Cuba) and Hispaniola (Santo Domingo), before returning to Spain. Columbus made four voyages to the New World between 1492 to 1502. As reported by some historians, the second, third and fourth trips took him to Hispaniola, Trinidad and Venezuela, and Mexico, respectively. According to many historians Columbus's shadow never fell on North America. So here we have a controversy. Today the Italians celebrate Columbus day here in America as America's Native American population mourn his arrival as an invader. What "many" historians say about Columbus is he introduced the "Americas" to Western Europe. So who really can make the case correctly that the Italians got it right that Columbus discovered North America, or was it the Indians who got it right that Columbus stole their ancestral lands? I guess it all depends on which historian you are listening to. Nevertheless a battle rages here in America that has caused the birth of the Indian historical grievance as they protest Columbus day by calling for the holiday to be changed to "Indigenous Peoples Day."

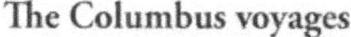
The Columbus voyages

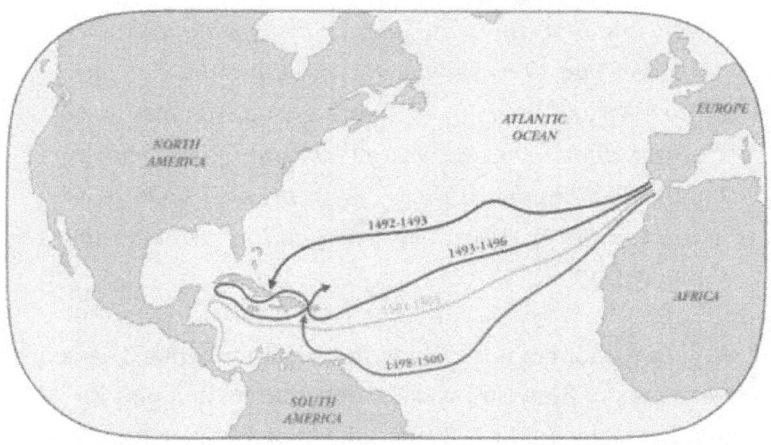

So how about throwing in another enduring multicultural event of the coming together of the Indian and the White man? Look no further than the Thanksgiving holiday Americans celebrates every November. What is taught in mainstream America is there was some sort of bountiful harvest in the 1600's and the Red man and the White man came together to celebrate it right? Well not according to the Lakota Indians. Seems they see this holiday in a different light. As reported on their website: http//www.republicoflakotah.com/ you will find their take on it in this article:

> *"The University of Connecticut: claims that the first Thanksgiving was not "a festive gathering of Indians and Pilgrims, but rather a celebration of the massacre of 700 Pequot men, women, and children. "In 1637 , the Pequot tribe of Connecticut gathered for their annual Green Corn Dance ceremony. Mercenaries of the English and Dutch surrounded and attacked their village burning down everything and shooting whoever tried to escape. The next day the Governor of the Massachusetts Bay Colony declared "a day*

> *of Thanksgiving, thanking God that they had eliminated over 700 of the Pequot tribe."* It was signed into law that, this day forth shall be a day of celebration and thanksgiving for subduing the Pequots. Most Americans believe Thanksgiving was this wonderful dinner and harvest celebration. The truth is the "Thanksgiving Dinner" was invented both to instill a false pride in Americans and to cover up the massacre."

I, as your author am not making the declaration that Thanksgiving was this massacre because I wasn't there and really don't know. I am only giving you the Lakotah's tribe take on it. Thanksgiving aside, the European did eventually make his way to the Northern continent and set up shop. Now here is that ideological liberal center I was talking about. The question to be considered is: How could a European discover a country that obviously was already discovered by the Indians by the fact that when the Pale Face landed he found the Indian here first? The simple answer is – he couldn't have, but with a – the continent was basically unknown at that time to the European and thus can be accurately assumed that once the white foot landed on the soil of the Northern continent it was "then" considered to be discovered by the European. The next question is what did the European discover on the continent that was to be eventually called North America? Was this a land governed by an organized nation of people? No. Was there any type of State buildings or at least something resembling a type of Government building on it? No. Was there any type of infrastructure that would leave the European explorers with the impression that they were invading a recognized defined country inhabited by a defined people within marked borders? No again. What these explorers did find was an undeveloped land inhabited by warring Indian tribes. Now these currently called Native Americans did not belong to a single Indian nation or even to a common tribe. In fact at that time there were estimated to be more than 160 tribes inhabiting territories from Alaska on down to Mexico and all the way to the east coast of this continent. These tribes all had different cultures and many had different languages. Not all these tribes lived in peace with each other and this is the key to the story. The historic reality of the Northern continent before the European set foot on it was that throughout history these tribes fought amongst themselves for many reasons but probably mostly for control of better hunting grounds. Some of these tribes even made alliances with these new incoming European arrivals because they saw them as potential allies against other tribes who were their long time enemies. The Cherokee actually allied with the French and fought the incoming English settlers. So the question just presents itself:

> *If the warring Indian tribes already on the continent had in their minds the legal right to make war with each other for better land and resources, could they legally or even morally be within their rights to make the claim that no one else was allowed to join the fight for better land and resources on the Northern continent?*

Further, if the Cherokee today can lodge an historical grievance against the European for historically invading his portion of hunting grounds in what is now several southern states, could they also lodge that same kind of grievance against another tribe if they had hypothetically invaded them say 50 years before the European landed? Surely no one is silly enough to think that all the Indian wars prior to the landing of the White man ended in a peaceful standstill. Some of those tribes had to have won some of those wars and with that victory came the control of the losing tribes hunting grounds. It's interesting that we never hear of any historical grievances against the winning tribes of those Indian wars isn't it? So was there some sort of continental agreement be it written or verbal between the Indian tribes that the land on this Northern continent was only to be fought over by themselves and no one else? I never heard of one. For the thinking person to suddenly make the claim that only Indians are allowed to fight and kill each other over land and resources on this continent is ridiculous on its own merit any way it can be presented. The historic reality that everyone wants to avoid is that the European basically landed on the shores here and joined the warring tribes in the historical battles and eventually ended up winning. Now no one is stupid enough to believe that the Red man should be happy about the outcome of this particular war, after all, who likes to lose? But it must be understood that the Europeans created the situation of acquiring an historical grievance within the borders of their newly conquered country by coming to an already inhabited continent in the first place, winning the wars with various Indian tribes, and then shoving them into reservations. But as history tells us, its' always up to the winners of wars to decide what to do with the losers after the war.

The worn out but still trusty White guilt mantra of "we took the land from the Indian" should be reconsidered because in truth, the White man didn't take anything from the Indian that some other tribe historically either already took, or lost, or at some time in the long past of the history of this continent just stumbled upon it as they wandered across the plains then chased other tribes away who tried to stumble upon it themselves at some point in time. Why can I say this? Because most Indian tribes pursued the nomadic lifestyle to follow the buffalo herds or they traveled to new hunting grounds in search of game to sustain themselves.

The entire Indian grievance can be summed up in three points:

1. The real problem here according to the various Indian tribes today is that they lost the war for the North American continent to the European.

2. After the historic European won the wars their offsprings have now allowed themselves to feel guilty over their ancestor's victory.
3. This new found guilt has provided the Indians with a platform to launch their historical grievance because the children of the conquering ancestors will now listen to it.

If the Indians had won the war with the European and chased him back across the Atlantic, these warring tribes would probably still be fighting each other today for the same reasons they always have if history is to be any judge. Basically the ideological mindset of the Indians and the liberals of today is that the Indians can hack each other to pieces till the end of time for better hunting grounds without an historical grievance or claiming foul, but once the blue eyed devils joined in the sin became defined in these two minds. We know the original conquering Europeans of America had no guilt or shame when they took this land for their people. It was a worthy conquest to them at that time. Today those ancestors are condemned as invading racists by many of the same people that enjoy the fruits of that historic conquest. I once was told by an American woman of Italian lineage that "we took the land from the Indians and we will always have this guilt." And so I replied back, "well then, if you truly feel so guilty about it then why don't you give your house to an Indian and go back to Italy?" Shocked, confused, and near slobbering, she replied, "I can't do that." And so I said, "then I guess you don't feel that guilty about it do you? It seems to me there are not too many pale faces here in America who feel that guilty at all about what was handed down to them by their ancestors. After all, it wasn't their spilt blood that paid for it was it? If the Whites in America truly feel guilty about their ancestors land conquest wouldn't they want to give it back? Does the word phony rise to the top of their afternoon cappuccino? To add to that I can say with much confidence that I haven't seen or heard of one guilt promoting White liberal professor ever advocating an exodus of himself and his white students back to their European countries of origin over this issue. Must be another reason these shameless losers are hanging around.

There are many Indian movements active today in America all promoting and serving the best interests of the various Indian nations. A few of the larger ones are listed here.

- Women of All Red Nations (WARN) was founded in 1978 in San Francisco, CA, and to date remains the most prominent activist Native American women's movement. WARN advocates for Native America Treaty Rights and for social, economic, and environmental justice for the Native American peoples.
- NCAI, the National Congress of American Indians, founded in 1944, is the oldest and largest and most representative American Indian and Alaska Native organization serving the broad interests of tribal governments and communities.
- LISN, the League of Indigenous Sovereign Nations. Their vision: Cultural survival envisions a future that respects and honors indigenous peoples inherent rights and dynamic cultures, deeply and richly interwoven in lands, languages, spiritual traditions, and artistic expression, rooted in self determination and self governance.

Although each group may have its own specific goal they are all fighting for the same basic principles of respect, their perceived rights, historic grievances, hatred for the Washington Redskins football team name, and self governance. What are they fighting against? If you're a pale face – you, and the type of government your ancestors formed. Now what does the existence of these organizations tell you? That a racial segment within the borders of this country has serious issues with how this country operates as it pertains to them.

Over a hundred years after the wars and forced relocation of the Red man off most his ancestral lands the American Indian still harbors an historical grievance. Personally I am not sure if it's fair to think that the Indian would be so forgetful. Something won by violence is never going to harbor a fond memory or an agreeable solution for the loser of the conflict. To use an analogy: If I knock your teeth out and take your watch are you ever going to be happy about what happened to your teeth and your watch? If I pass this watch on to my son and your son sees it on his wrist and knows it was once his fathers and knows how his father lost that watch, do you think your son will ever have fond memories of how that watch ended up in my sons family? That is a microcosm of an historical grievance. A perceived historic wrong committed in the eyes of a victim is one that will be nurtured and passed on. This nurturing can cause the perceived wrong to take on a life of its own which will eventually end up being a perpetual thorn in the cultural side of the dominant host nation.

We all know that through the ages that wars have been fought over land. I personally am not here to tell anyone that all wars are wrong and all land taken by conquering armies is anti-Christian. It's just a fact of life that these events have happened and will continue to happen from time to time on this rock. So what's a conqueror to do? Well if he's a Christian conqueror he should be seeking guidance from the good book. What did Gods conquerors do? Look no further than in the book of Judges when Joshua was tasked with taking the land God had sworn to give to Israel. But Israels failure to obey God's specific orders on "how" to conquer the land caused greed to set in the tribes of Israel after the passing of this great military leader during this campaign. This failure was so devastating to the future of Israel that God sent one of His angels to speak to the people about it.

Judges 2:1,

> *Now the angel of the LORD came up from Gilgal to Bochim. And he said, "I brought you up out of Egypt and led you into the land which I have sworn to your fathers; and I said, 'I will never break My covenant*

with you, **2**, *and as for you, you shall make no covenant with the inhabitants of this land; you shall tear down their altars.' But you have not obeyed Me; what is this you have done?* **3**, *"Therefore I also said, 'I will not drive them out before you; but they will become as thorns in your sides and their gods will be a snare to you.'"* **4**, *When the angel of the LORD spoke these words to all the sons of Israel, the people lifted up their voices and wept.*

Just what was Israel's transgression? Look no further than back in Chapter 1 of Judges.

Judges 1:21,

And the children of Benjamin did not drive out the Jeb'usites that inhabited Jerusalem; but the Jeb'usites dwell with the children of Benjamin in Jerusalem unto this day.

Judges 1:27,

Neither did Manas'seh drive out the inhabitants of Beth–she'an and her towns, nor Ta'anach and her towns, nor the inhabitants of Dor and her towns, nor the inhabitants of Ib'le-am and her towns, nor the inhabitants of Megid'do and her towns: but the Canaanites would dwell in that land.

Judges 1:29,

Neither did E'phra-im drive out the Canaanites that dwelt in Gezer; but the Canaanites dwelt in Gezer among them.

Judges 1: 30,

Neither did Zeb'ulun drive out the inhabitants of Kitron, nor the inhabitants of Na'halol; but the Canaanites dwelt among them, and became tributaries.

Judges 1:31,

Neither did Asher drive out the inhabitants of Accho, nor the inhabitants of Zidon, nor of Ahlab, nor of Achzib, nor of Helbah, nor of Aphik, nor of Rehob: **32,** *but the Ash'erites dwelt among the Canaanites, the inhabitants of the land: for they did not drive them out.*

Judges 1:33,

Neither did Naph'tali drive out the inhabitants of Beth–she'mesh, nor the inhabitants of Beth–a'nath; but he dwelt among the Canaanites, the inhabitants of the land: nevertheless, the inhabitants of Beth–she'mesh and of Beth–a'nath became tributaries unto them.

How come Israel did not obey God's will and drive out the conquered inhabitants of the land? God was prepared to deliver the promised land into their hands and He had prepared Israel for this conquest.
Judges 1:28,

> *And it came to pass, when Israel was strong, that they put the Canaanites to tribute, and did not utterly drive them out.*

Lets have another look at what the Lord's angel told Israel. **Judges 2:3,**

> *Wherefore I also said, I will not drive them out from before you; but they shall be as thorns in your sides, and their gods shall be a snare unto you.*

The message is clear. God wanted His people to conquer the promised land and separate from the conquered inhabitants by driving them out of the land. So apply this bible message to America's Indian historical grievance. If the conquering Europeans drove out the Indians and removed them from the Northern continent by say driving them either up into Canada or down into Mexico there would be no Indian historical grievance within the borders of America would there? Now I am not advocating driving out the Indians from America today but what I am saying is God in His infinite wisdom knows if His people are dwelling with foreigners, these same foreigners will eventually end up being thorns in His peoples sides and/or His people will end up worshiping other gods like what happened to Solomon. So can it be disputed that Christianity in America is under relentless attack by non-Christians and foreigners today? Is this a thorn in the Christians side?

Grievance #2
~ The Mexicans lost the war but made some coin anyway ~

The Mexican-American War was an armed conflict originating from the wake of the 1845 annexation of Texas which lasted from 1846 to 1848. Once again the White European was on the march for more territory and the Mexicans were not laying down. Well as the story goes the U.S. claimed victory in 1848. The treaty of Guadalupe-Hildago was negotiated by a Nicholas Trist whereby Mexico ceded to the United States the territories of Upper California, present day Arizona, New Mexico, Utah, Nevada, and Colorado. Mexico also relinquished all claims to Texas and recognized the Rio Grande as the southern boundary with the United States. In return Mexico received $15 million dollars for their trouble. Well as all historical grievances go this one is no exception. Today Mexican children are taught in school that Texas was stolen from them by those Americans in that historic Yankee war of aggression in 1846.

So today we in America have a disgruntled neighbor just south of our border who is still resentful of the loss of their territory by conquest and cash. But if one takes a closer look at the distorted history of Mexico itself, it seems they also have a few skeletons in their own closet that they are still dealing with. Looking back in history it seems Spain had a conquest involving the native population of South America a number of centuries ago. History tells us that Spain conquered territories involving Mexico and other parts of South America while also acquiring many of their women for the glory of the Spanish empire. So are these conquering Spanish Mexicans of today the same bunch who wouldn't kindly support the Yankee secession of Texas? Well to begin to answer my own question, a Mexican is a racial cross between an Indian and a European Spaniard. But just how did this cross racial mixture come about? You are going to have to go way back for this one and give credit to that Spanish guy named Cortes. It seems around the early 1500's the Spanish conquest of the Aztec empire was one of the most important campaigns in the Spanish colonization of the Americas at that time.

The invasion began in 1519 and was claimed victorious for Spain in 1521 by a coalition army of Spanish Conquistadors led by Hernan Cortes and Indian Tlaxcalan warriors led by Xicotencatl the Younger. Referring to the *Wiki* file, in the 16th century around 240,000 Spanish soldiers entered the South American ports. They were joined by

450,000 more Spanish troops in the next century. Unlike the migrating English "married" colonists of North America, the majority of these Spanish colonists were single military men who ended up copulating with the local natives. The result of these sexual unions created the vast class of people historically known as Mestizos. This term refers specifically to those people of the particular racial mixture of Spanish European and South America Indian who now inhabit and comprise much of the population of Latin America. Thus the years went by and voila, today we have a country just south of the American border called Mexico that is now filled with people called Mexicans.

Today the original racial Indians who still live in Mexico have an historical grievance of their own against these modern day Mestitos now called Mexicans who rule Mexico today. The movement of these grievance holding Indians is called: The Zapatista National Liberation Army (EZLN). It is a revolutionary leftist political and militant group based in the Chiapas, the most southern state of Mexico. In 1994 this group declared war against the Mexican State for its military, paramilitary, and corporate incursions into Chiapas. The war was primarily defensive. In recent years this conflict has focused on a strategy of civil resistance. Today the rebellion remains a work in progress having established complete political and economic autonomy, the Zapatistas govern and police their own communities across five regions of Chiapas. Relations with the Mexican Country remains strained and the Zapatistas complain of regular harassment by State, military, and paramilitary forces, that surround their territory. The Zapatistas especially take issue against the oppression that this Mexican reign has wrought on the "original people" of the territories Mexico.

This official statement from the Zapatistas says it all.

> "*We are the dispossessed millions....and our enemies are the wealthy and the state* (read Mexican State) *that have oppressed Mexican Indian nationals for at*

least 70 years and the indigenous people for the last 500 years."

Well, well, well, what have we here? Did I just stumble upon some type of Mexican oppression of an indigenous people for the last 500 years over stolen land? Lets see if I can add those numbers up. 2016 take away 500 equals....yep, that puts us squarely in the early 1500's. Funny how that was exactly when the Spanish conquest of South America began wasn't it? The Zapatistas argue that attempting change through all legal means has been rendered unsuccessful for many years by the Mexican PRI dictatorship and therefore they have referred to article 39 of the Mexican constitution which states that, "the people have, at all times, the inalienable right to alter or abolish the form of their own government."

http://www.constituteproject.org/constitution/Mexico 2007.pdf

And indeed it does say that in Title II Chapter 1 of the Mexican Constitution.

So as the Mexicans of today claim foul for the loss of their territory to the U.S., the original inhabitants of Mexico are also claiming foul against the historical Spaniards, turned Mestitos, today called Mexicans, for the historical oppression of their people and for the loss of their land. Another Corona with that tangled web Pancho?

For well over one hundred years the Mexicans in the U.S. and from Mexico still have an historical grudge against America and like the Native Americans they are actively working to take back a chunk of real estate through their own movement called – The Chicano movement. Affiliated groups such as La Raza and the Brown Berets lead the way. La Raza, by the way means, "The Race." The Mexican Race that is. This organizations founding document, "el Plan Espiritual de Aztland" condemns the brutal gringo invasion of their territories and urges Hispanics to reclaim the land of their birth while declaring that the call of their blood is their power, their responsibility, and their inevitable destiny. It appears to the Mexican that it's all about blood isn't it? Ponder that statement for a moment....

Now, for the sake of seeing how that famous American egalitarianism works, let me try an experiment. Let's say I decide to form a group similar to La Raza, only this groups membership will only be for White people. Inspired by the Mexican groups name, I'll call mine also "The Race." So what if I said the exact same thing in my mission statement that La Raza said. That "Blood is our Power and our Destiny." Can I tell you that after you read that statement you immediately pictured in your mind a bunch of White racists in Nazi uniforms waving Confederate Flags didn't you? Do you find it odd that when I asked you to ponder that same statement a minute ago as it pertained to the Mexican group "La Raza" you didn't have those same knee jerk racist thoughts? By the way did I tell you I am a mind reader? To continue on, say I decided to hold a convention and began to call on those same sponsors that La Raza had for their convention. Do you think Home Depot, McDonalds, Toyota, Walmart, and the Miller Brewing Company, will sponsor my White race convention too? Will Hillary Clinton and Karl Rove sign up as speakers for my convention as they did for the La Raza convention? Need some more time to think about that one? Is it an accepted truism in America that when people of Mexican blood, or even when any of the minorities of color in this country get together and do something for their race it is viewed as positive by the media and even by this country's population in general? Is it just as true if White people did the same for their race that it would be viewed as negative and racist? Does this mean there is good blood and bad blood in multicultural America today? Just doesn't sound very egalitarian to me at all.

Grievance #3
~ Will those Blacks ever stop enslaving their own people? ~

I don't think there is a more racially charged issue in America today than "historic Black slavery." Past slavery in this country has been used to cause resentment for some and gain wealth for others as well as produce guilt and empty pockets for some others. Let's face it, as long as Whitey can be kept in the racial guilt outhouse by the slavery promoters, the money and power will continue to roll in on the racist gravy train. But there are a couple of questions just under the corner of the slavery rug that those race promoters seem to side step and conveniently scoot around. Those questions would be:

1. Who were the original slave owners of our Black citizens from Africa?
2. Who continues this unusual practice today?

Let's look at the first question. Putting the old Hollywood series "Roots" in the fiction category where it belongs, White slave traders historically sailed to Africa not to spend their time chasing down natives around the bush with a rope, but actually to buy the Negros already in bondage from the powerful African tribal chieftains. Now lets examine this statement of mine. Look at the word "buy." If you buy something from someone that can only mean that the person selling the item had to have owned it in the first place otherwise how could they sell it to you? You can't sell your neighbors car out from under him can you? So can we not say for the sake of historical reality that the White slave traders "bought" their slaves from the "original slave owners" in Africa who were – Black?

In Hugh Thomas's book, "*The Slave Trade*", and Robin Blackburn's book, "*The making of New World Slavery*" they both shed some new light on centuries of slave trading in the African continent. What these authors uncovered was that the African slave trade flourished in the early middle ages, as early as 869, especially between Muslim traders and the western African Kingdoms. For moralists the most important aspect of that trade should be that Muslims were selling goods to African Kingdoms and the African Kings were paying with skin. In most trades no violence was necessary to obtain those slaves. What we can glean from these two authors is that there was an active slave industry well established on the African continent between Muslims and the African tribes as far back as the Middle Ages and that would have been centuries before the European ever landed on that same continent.

Moving forward in history to bypass legends, novels, and Hollywood movies, it was over 700 years later when twenty Africans were brought to America's shores by a Dutch soldier and sold to the English as slaves. The year was 1619. These Dutch slave traders did not need to savagely kill entire tribes in order to exact tribute in slaves. All they needed to do was bring goods that appealed to the chiefs from those African tribes that were active in the skin trade. From trading war captives and criminals, to sometimes their own kin, the African slave industry was lucrative and booming with the Muslims and then much later with the Europeans as regards to this peculiar business. When Britain abolished the peculiar practice in 1807, it not only had to contend with opposition from White slavers but also from the African kings who had become accustomed to the wealth gained from selling their slaves and also from taxes collected on slaves that passed through their domain. In the article: *Origins of the African Slave Trade*, by Piero Scaruffi, he tells us "In 1820 the king of the African kingdom of Ashanti inquired why the Christians did not want to trade slaves with him anymore since they worshiped the same God as the Muslims and these Muslims were continuing the trade. By the time the slave trade was abolished in the West there were many more slaves in Africa owned by Africans than in the Americas. Inevitably abolition in the West meant many African states hitherto dependent on the slave trade faced severe economic disruption. One result was that slavery in Africa actually increased in the 19th century."

Let's be fair though. Just because it was the African chiefs who sold their slaves to anyone with the right goods one cannot assume that their Negro slaves liked being part of the transaction any better. But that being said, one begins to wonder why here in America its citizens are educated to believe that the only place on earth that seemed to have had the institution of slavery was Dixie. According to Leslie Harris, a professor of History at Emory University, he goes on record saying, "more New Yorkers owned slaves than all the Whites in the Antebellum South. We need to acknowledge that our history is more complicated than a benighted racist South and a free North."

http://history.emory.edu/home/people/faculty/harris-leslie.html.

Lorenzo Johnson Greene, writes in his article, *"The Negro in Colonial New England,"* Whether it was officially encouraged, as in New York and New Jersey, or not as in Pennsylvania, the slave trade flourished in Colonial Northern ports in the 1700's. But New England was by far the leading slave merchant of the American Colonies. Even after slavery was outlawed in the North, ships out of New England continued to carry thousands of African slaves to the American South."

http://scholarworks.umb.edu/trotte rreview /vol3/iss1/5/

But the prevailing attitude the historically ignorant have in America is to continue to keep their index finger pointing southward when engaging in slavery verbalize. Let neither history nor reality get in the way of America's delusional conclusion on who economically benefited from slavery in this country.

Now that we have fielded the first question of *who were the original slave owners of our Black citizens from Africa*, how about that second question. *Who continues this unusual practice today?*

It is well documented that all nations in the West officially banned slavery in the 1800's with Brazil being the last in 1888. So to find our answer to the above question might we look over the pond towards Africa once again? In an article by Ricco Siasoco, called *Modern Slavery*, "he goes on to point out that sometimes referred to as bonded laborers (because of the debts owed to their masters) public perception of modern slavery is often confused with reports of workers in low wage jobs or inhumane working conditions. However, modern day slaves differ from these workers because they are actually held in physical bondage as they are shackled, held at gun point, etc. These modern day slaves can be found laboring as servants or concubines in the Sudan, as child carpet slaves in India, or as cane cutters in Haiti." In an article on December 23, 2009, in *Port-au-Prince*, Haiti, it says, "poverty has forced at least 225,000 children in Haiti's cities into slavery as unpaid household servants." The *Pan American Development Foundation's* report also said, "some of those children, mostly young girls suffer sexual and psychological abuse toiling in extreme hardship." According to *Anti-Slavery International*, the worlds oldest rights organization, "there are currently over 20 million people in bondage today." Now where will you geographically find those places that continue the practice of modern slavery? Not in the West.

Can I make the claim that if the slave reparations crowd in America are not greedy or disingenuous, they are at least historically ignorant. If these Blacks in America today really want to blame someone for America's past slavery maybe they should be blaming their slave trading ancestors who put them up for sale in the first place. Maybe they should be asking themselves why some of their own kin from the old country still are participating in such a peculiar practice today? Lastly, maybe our African American citizens should be also asking themselves if they are better off here in America than they would be in Africa today? Those are the real questions that the race crowd in this country have a great financial motivation to avoid today.

So there you have it. Black Africans selling Black African slaves back then and Black Africans selling Black African slaves today. Can it be said that some things never change? I will make the statement that this historical grievance against White America for its past slavery of Blacks is stronger today that it was a hundred years ago for the reason of all the money involved. After all, big checks are a great motivator to continue to exploit this past grievance isn't it? Can I say that all Blacks harbor an historical grievance against America for past slavery? No. I'm sure there are those who don't but my point is that the prevailing ideology of slavery in America being promoted by the Blacks, the liberal news media, and the U.S. Government, is victim-hood. That this victim-hood in their mind is caused by their historical slavery in America. It must be understood that Blacks who believe they are a victim or promote victim-hood for past slavery "are not" claiming to be victims of their ancestors who originally owned them first and sold them later. They are only claiming to be victims of the buyers of the historic transaction. According to the U.S. Government, the Public Schools, the Media, and the race hustlers, todays Negro is a victim of an historical social injustice as a people because of their past slavery in this country. And this has caused some to make the claim that they are owed financial reparations from the purchasers of the original slavery transaction. Do African Americans believe their slave selling ancestors owe them reparations? I never heard it claimed or reported.

History has shown that the Black race when living in their own countries of origin on balance have always taken the low road with regards to the issue of slavery. But nevertheless the slave past of the Black American is an historical grievance that continues to this day within the larger Black population in this country.

~ Conclusison ~

All three of these discussed grievances held by the Indians, the Mexicans, and the Blacks, encompass over 100 million people and each have held on to that grievance for more than one hundred years. These grievances are continually acted upon to this day by the holders through the creation of organizations, protests, and pursuing financial gain of one sort or another for the reason of historic victim-hood. The first two listed entities that hold grievances will never go away until a chunk of real estate has been carved up and out of the U.S. and handed over, or in their minds handed back to the possessors of those grievances. The third seeks continual reparations.

It must be understood that the combining of two different racial cultures in one country must naturally result in the lowering of one and the elevation of the other for the very reason that no two cultures are exactly alike. The culture that has geographically combined with another by winning a war or by overwhelming the other by mass immigration will usually and/or eventually dictate to the other what the prevailing cultural norms and standards in traditional society will be within the borders of the shared region. The unavoidable result of having one races cultural norms being relegated to a subclass by the more successful race can cause the consequential birth of that phenomenon called: The historical grievance.

MULTICULTURALISM AND THE MILITARY

So whats the advantage of having a multicultural army? I wouldn't ask Texas that question for awhile. We have already talked about the Ft. Hood non-terrorist incident committed by an individual who the Army put in charge of the *mental health* of our troops. American born, American educated, and a member of our Armed Forces, nevertheless when the time came to choose sides, religion and blood prevailed over citizenship and the U.S. Constitution. Now was this a unique incident? Not hardly. Unfortunately there have been other incidents of this kind in the U.S. Military.

Back in the 2003 invasion of Iraq, U.S. Army sergeant Hasan Akbar (born Mark Fidel Kools) from Watts, CA, was convicted for the double murder of two officers and wounding fourteen others of the 327th Infantry Regiment. Mark Kools was renamed Hasan by his mother after she remarried and converted to Islam. Akbar himself reportedly said just moments after his arrest, "you guys are coming into our countries and you're going to rape our women and kill our children."

Then on June 1, 2009 in Little Rock, Arkansas, a Muslim convert named Abdulhakim Muhammad aka Carlos Bledsoe was charged with fatally shooting one American soldier and wounding another at a military recruiting center. Abdulhakim said he didn't consider the killing murder because the U.S. Military action in the Middle East made the killing justified.

~ Loyalty, bombs, and God ~

Currently there is an estimated 15,000 Muslims in the ranks of the U.S. Military. As America continues her quest for yet even more diversity shouldn't we be asking ourselves the question: What are the chances of another American citizen jihad against American soldiers? Shouldn't those responsible in our Army be asking themselves that question as they irresponsibly call these terrorist attacks – non-terrorist attacks? According to *alllgov.com,* today there are more than 100,000 foreign immigrants serving in the U.S. Military, a full 8% of the entire armed forces. Just how loyal are these non-citizens who must still have strong family ties to their original homelands? "In response to a survey of newly naturalized citizens in Los Angeles, 90% of Muslim immigrants said that if there were a conflict between the U.S. and their country of origin they would be inclined to support their country of origin" as reported by John Fonte of the *Hudson Institute*. Surprised? You shouldn't be. To the Muslim it's all about God and blood. The two most powerful elements in the psyche of the human being. It's a natural concept and the Muslim is not a confused person at all. They clearly know who they are and what they stand for. For in the country of America today there is no blood, no religion, no language, and no common set of values, no unifying history, or no unifying culture, that helps to tell the American citizen who he is and what he stands for because, hey, we're multicultural. We don't need those outdated concepts do we? Unlike the other races in America, the White American clings to the only thing he has left to explain himself and that would be his Constitution. White knuckling this document he will proudly proclaim to his fellow citizens of all races "are we not all brothers in our ideology according to this founding document?" All I can say to that is Fort Hood, Texas, November 5.

History is replete with examples of Generals with mercenaries in their ranks with no national loyalty who fought for plunder and that alone. While the mercenary is not exactly an immigrant soldier in the current American Army, there are some solid comparisons that can be made. It stands to reason that the immigrant soldier cannot have the same loyalty the legal citizen soldier has because like the merc, the main motivation at least for a duration can only be money. After all he is not in the war to protect his homeland or to use the catch phrase of America today "to fight for his country's freedom" is he? This missing connection creates a kind of paradox of allegiances while the immigrant soldier finds himself saying "if I die here, I am not even dying for my country." While fighting in America's wars can put the immigrant soldier on a path to citizenship, it still makes his fellow soldiers wonder just how trustworthy he will be in a dangerous situation. For the immigrant soldier the ethical lines are not always clear. Unfortunately the last thing an American soldier wants to consider during a hot fire fight is the current loyalty status of the immigrant soldier watching his back.

~ Todays ally, tomorrows enemy ~

History tells us that this statement above can happen sooner than one wishes to consider. There was a time when Saddam Hussein was our guy in the Middle East. It was just over three decades ago that America found itself on Iraq's side during the Iran-Iraq war which was fought from 1980 to 1988. President Ronald Reagan during that time decided that the U.S. Could not afford to allow Iraq to lose the war and said that we would do whatever was necessary to prevent that from happening. Yet just two years after the end of that war which ended in a stalemate America invaded this same Iraq and ended up fighting the very same dictator that we backed in his war with Iran.

Looking backwards just two years from the beginning of the Iran-Iraq war there are those who remember that famous toast President Jimmy Carter gave in 1978 on New Years Eve to the then Shah of Iran in which he said, "under the Shah's brilliant leadership Iran is an island of stability in one of the most troublesome regions of the world. There is no other state figure that I could appreciate and like more." But only one year later our strongest ally in the Middle East was overthrown and sent to live in exile after the 1979 Iranian revolution. Today Iran is now viewed as a nuclear threat. So if history is any judge, the saying of "todays ally may be tomorrows enemy" is not a policy the American government abides by, believes in, or even pretends to understand, in its eternal quest for yet more diversity.

In *Adrian Morgans 2007 article*: Australia: Muslim mercenaries or traitors? "The issue of Muslim Australians fighting abroad has been highlighted in the case of an Australian born fellow nicknamed Jihad Jack, aka Joseph Thomas, a Melbourne taxi driver and a convert to Islam. He left Oz and had gone to Afghanistan to take part in the insurgency. He had attended the Al-Faroq training camp and had fought on the front lines for about a week. In 2006, Jihad Jack was caught and convicted of receiving funds from Al Qaeda. In addition to Australia's woes, another incident involving two more Australians were arrested with other foreign nationals suspected of smuggling weapons to Somalia. And now comes the latest round of concerns about the Australian identity problems being pitted against Muslim values involving a one Sheikh Taj Din al-Hilali of Lakemba Mosque in Sydney. The Sheikh compared women who did not wear Muslim coverings to uncovered meat left out for cats. As Mr. Morgan writes, this has caused the confused Australians for the last two years to engage in a debate over whether immigrant Muslims truly wish to integrate with the Australian culture." Hey, I'm confused, aren't you?

Rep. Ron Paul from Texas has it right about the Muslim connection in this supposed American war on terror. He says "they are here because we are over there." With America and England leading the war on terror in the Middle East are we not actually galvanizing the Muslim world into a war for the total defense of their race and religion? Before 911 America backed Israel in every engagement against the Palestinians. We backed the regime of the Shah of Iran against his own people before he was overthrown by a populist uprising in 1979.

We bombed Libya in 1986 and invaded it in 2011. We backed Iraq in a war with Iran in the 80's. We attacked Iraq in 1990. We bombed the Sudan in 1998. We bombed Afghanistan in 1998. After 911 we are still in Iraq and now fighting the longest war in American history in Afghanistan. Is anyone still confused as to why these Muslims are being galvanized against what they call the great Satan? The issue is clear to the Muslim world. When Muslims are being killed its usually by the weapon of an American or Brit.

Do we really want to pursue this type of war with the type of people God has described in the bible as being a "wild man?" In Genesis, the birth of the Arab Nation begins with Abraham taking the servant Hagar, his wife's Sarai's (Sarah) maid to acquire an heir. After the birth of Ishmael, Abraham and Hagar's son, Sarah ends up in a family way. This along with Hagar's bad attitude caused a conflict that eventually forced Hagar to have to leave and it was here when God sent an angel to Hagar. In the King James Bible it played out like this:
Gen. 16:10,

> *And the angel of the Lord said unto her* (Hagar) *I will multiply thy seed exceedingly , that it shall not be numbered for the multitude.* 11, *And the angel of the LORD said unto her, Behold, thou art with child, and shalt bear a son, and shalt call his name Ish'ma-el; because the LORD hath heard thy affliction* 12, *And he will be a wild man; his hand will be against every man, and every man's hand against him: and he shall dwell in the presence of all his brethren.*

Just to add some more weight to the characteristic description of the Arab, there is a little Arab fable that's often used to explain the Middle Eastern man:

"One day a frog and a scorpion were standing by the river bank. They both wanted to get across to the other side. The frog can swim but the scorpion cannot. So the scorpion asks the frog to carry him across. But, protests the frog, If I let you on my back you will sting me. Don't worry, says the scorpion. Why would I do that since if I sting you I will drown. This makes sense to the frog and he lets the scorpion climb on his back and proceeds to jump into the water and starts swimming across the river. Halfway across the scorpion does indeed sting the frog. As they both sink down into the depth the frog speaks his last words, "why did you do that, now we will both die!" The scorpion shrugs his carapace and says, "I cannot help myself, this is the Middle East."

Does this sound like something a wild man would say? Does this sound like a corner of the world we want to be militarily involved in? Shouldn't we be thinking about taking Ron Paul's advice and just leave these people alone?

~ Does America read the writing on the wall? ~

Back in the Vietnam War, America had its own problems with its multicultural Army. It was said by some in the Black leadership during that war that Blacks were being killed disproportionately more than Whites because....yes, you guessed it. Racism. According to the Vietnam War Statistics site there were:

88.4% of the men who served in Vietnam were White.
86.3% of the men who died in Vietnam were White.

While....

10.6% of the men who served in Vietnam were Black.
12.5% of the men who died in Vietnam were Black.

These statistics should clear up any complaints by the Black leadership during that war but just the fact that those complaints were taken seriously shows how deep multiculturalism can cut into the psyche of a nation. There have been other incidents that have manifested themselves in this country during times of war involving other races that weren't Black like the Japanese interment during World War II. I'm sure the internment was not the most popular decision the country had to make during that war but the survival of the nation must be assured and political correctness be damned. Can any thinking individual claim after the attack on Pearl Harbor that there was not going to be a major trust issue coming into focus with regards to the Japanese Americans? I mean can you imagine a Japanese citizen serving in the Pentagon during that war? Or to use a more recent example, how about a Soviet holding a cabinet position in the White House during the Cold War? The undeniable fact is when America was more of a Christian European nation it had much less trouble making critical and unpopular decisions to protect its citizens during times of war. Today multicultural America finds itself in a racial quagmire when considering military conflicts. This causes it to socially freeze like a deer in the headlights when having to consider offending one portion of its population at the risk of placing the rest in mortal danger.

So what if America suddenly decided to go to war against say Mexico for whatever reason? Just sit on that for a moment. Maybe you will need to contemplate how many Mexican American citizens are in our Army. Then you might want to think about how many Mexican immigrants are in our Army. Then you might want to think about how many Mexican citizens are living in America today. Then you might want to think about how many Mexican illegal aliens are currently in America. Now add all that up and take a guess how this one will turn out. How many Mexicans do you personally know would attack their original homeland? Can you guess what word rhymes with magilla and then tack on the word "war" behind it? To the Mexican it's all about blood and soil. Just ask La Raza.

To further prove my point, for those who were there. Who can forget that infamous soccer game in 1998 in Los Angeles with the U.S. Against Mexico at the Coliseum? The Mexican fans were overwhelmingly pro-Mexico even though most of them lived in the U.S. They booed during the National Anthem as they held U.S. Flags upside down. Coach Steve Sampson reported, "as the match progressed, supporters of the U.S. Team were insulted, pelted with projectiles, punched and spat upon. Beer and trash was thrown at the U.S. Players before and after the match. The coach of the U.S. Team said, "this was the most painful experience I have ever had in the profession." Well what were you expecting coach? The Mexicans to support a team which represents the country they still believe stole a good chunk of their ancestral lands?

Look, White people on balance do not understand that to other races in the world there are more important things in life than money and materialism. This noble thought that other people hold their blood higher than money literally causes a short circuit in many white brains. The White American has been so successfully socially engineered by the multicultural elites to reject his own blood connection with his people that he eventually comes to believe everyone is just as socially engineered as himself. This is the reason for the White man's constant state of confusion about race issues currently dividing America today. How many more racial and/or terrorist incidents need to happen before Mr. Snow White's brain re-connects the circuits to receive the understanding that – blood is stronger than an ideology written on a piece of paper?

I am sorry to inform you Mr. Middle Class White American but you are probably the only one who truly believes in that Constitution you hold so dear to your heart. Don't tell me your elected representatives in D.C. believe in it. These elites don't believe in the Constitution you believe in. They believe in something they call a "Living Constitution." This means that the document in question is in the continual state of metamorphosis as it magically changes into whatever they need and desire to promote their agenda at any given time.

The majority of the Black population's belief in the Constitution is balanced out with their historical grievance. The American Jew, American Muslim, American Mexican, and Native Americans on balance are known to lean towards blood and their country of origin in times of uncertainty. I am not blaming them or pointing my index finger at them. I am merely pointing out the obvious conflicting loyalties that multiculturalism breeds. The American Indian has had a very unique experience with written legal documents in their history. They'll show blood first. I would even include Asian Americans to a certain degree with sticking with their own first just by witnessing the small exclusive enclaves they create in this country with many still writing Asian characters on their places of business which the typical American cannot understand. The simple reason for this is that these people of other races all have something Whitey no longer has and that is they still possess a spiritual, emotional, historical, and physical connection to their blood. To them blood is thicker than ink. It has a more meaningful history to them than a piece of paper with some words written on it. It is a part of them that can be touched, loved, and uniquely claimed as their own. I am not saying the American Constitution is bad. What I am saying is when the only thing you have left to hold a multicultural country together is a document written by some White guys over two hundred years ago, your country's cultural glue will be a mile wide and one inch deep. Why will the cultural glue be only one inch deep? Because all the other natural elements that were present in the original God created organic cultures are missing. The American Constitutionalist cannot count on religion to assist his Constitution to hold the people together. There are too many different religions here. He cannot count on the country's racial breakdown to help. He cannot count on a common language to unite the communication between his fellow citizens when bilingualism and even multilingualism is advocated and promoted in this country. He cannot count on a common unifying history. The hapless Constitutionalist cannot even count on an agreed set of customs and values to help. The simple reason for this is because his now living Constitution tells him that all the worlds values and beliefs are equal to his own and must be fully protected in his now multicultural country. What this "man created" ideological thinking has done is create a collage of competing races and ethnicities within a common border. All the "God created" natural elements in our once organic culture used to be here. We were once a Christian European country whose founding documents were all written by Christian Europeans. The Black minority was Christianized into the European culture, and the Indians were tucked away separately in the reservations. Christianity was our religion and English was our language. But enter the elite multiculturalist forcing his "man made" ideology upon the people of America and voila – the result is all you have left to hold the American people together is a document even your elite masters don't believe in.

So what's a country to do? Why have your multicultural America support dual citizenship of course! Most of America's dual citizens are Mexican Americans. Dave Ray, Communications Director for the Federation for American Immigration Reform, writes in *Worldnetdaily*, "In Mexico, which had previously discouraged dual citizenship, passed a law declaring that any person born in Mexico, or born to Mexican nationals wherever they reside, can claim Mexican citizenship even if they are citizens of another country. A more recent law now permits absentee voting in Mexican elections. The upshot of these changes is that millions of Hispanics could be eligible to vote in Mexico's elections as well as U.S. Elections. There are now a growing number of U.S. Citizens whose umbilical cord is attached to the Mexican government. That will have huge political ramifications in upcoming U.S. Domestic policy debates, particularly in immigration and trade."

Check out the question below from an American soldier (in his own words) from the U.S. Internet site which assists people with dual American citizenship issues.

Www.justanswer.com/law/immigration

> *"I have dual citizenship (Russian American) I currently serving in the U.S. Army, and I'm 21 years old. My question is can I go to Russia without a problem? I did not serve the Russian Army, and I left Russia when I was 15. My Russian passport expired. What do I need for visa? Thank you for your help."*

I know the American Army doesn't care but I personally would like to know where this soldiers loyalty would fall if America went to war with Russia.

~ There is no such thing as a man with two fathers ~

In his article: *When Conflict Focuses on Citizenship*, Frances Stead Sellers writes: "War is all about taking sides. It all plays into nationality, ethnicity, your birthplace, and the place you lived as an adult. What is most important is whom you identify with in the times of conflict. A dual citizen, according to the U.S. State Departments definition is: ….owing allegiance to both the United States and the foreign country of a persons origin. Dual citizenship upsets the traditional link between citizenship and allegiance to one nation."

It is unrealistic to suppose that immigrants ever simply switched allegiance the moment they moved from one country to another. The U.S. Army today doesn't keep track of how many dual citizens there are in its ranks according to S. Douglas Smith, Public Affairs Office at the U.S. Army Recruiting Command. He goes on to say, "All enlistees take an oath of allegiance to the Constitution and dual citizenship only becomes an issue if they apply for jobs that require special security clearance."

Some of us are probably familiar with the story of that infamous traitor, Jonathon Pollard, who was an American-Israeli citizen who worked for the U.S. Navy. His claim to fame was that he stole more military secrets in the 1980's from the U.S. than any other spy in American history. During his interrogation, Pollard said he felt compelled to put the interests of what he called "my State Israel" ahead of his own country America. Sounds like one of those blood is thicker than water things doesn't it? As a Navy counter-intelligence specialist this dual citizen had top secret clearance.

Zooming forward to witness the amazing learning curve of the U.S. Military: A U.S. Naval flight officer with extensive signals intelligence background was accused by the Service of passing secrets to China, the *USNI News* reported on April 11, 2016. Lt. Cmdr. Edward C. Lin, 39, who served on some of the Navy's most sensitive intelligence gathering aircraft, faces several counts of espionage and other charges. He was originally a Taiwanese national before his family moved to the U.S. Gotta love that dual thing.

So there you have again the classic case of a soldier feeling compelled to choose sides even when a war was not going on between his two countries. Put in the right position the damage a soldier with dual citizenship can cause can be catastrophic. A wise man once said, *"a man cannot be the son of two fathers."* Jesus Himself tries to lend some divine inspiration on this matter that I feel can be applied to this dual citizenship issue in Matthew 6:24, *"No man can serve two masters."* Can this scripture apply to the statement, "no man can serve two countries equally? If a compromising situation arises where the dual citizen must make a choice on which side of a war he will be on, it is assured that the dual citizen will choose one side over the other.

~ Kill the inhuman, it's only the enemy ~

So how about that little thing every country must do to the enemy before they play war with them. You know, dehumanize them. "The secret to propaganda is that when you demonize, you dehumanize" said *James Forsher*, a film historian and documentary maker. On the site: *Iraq Veterans against the War:* One soldier on the site explains "the abuse of the Iraqis is not the result of people waking up one morning as monsters, but it is part of military culture. They train us that way. He also says the brutality comes from being told that people are out to kill you. You must remove the humanity from the enemy to make it easier to oppress them, to brutalize them, to beat them, and in doing so you remove the humanity from yourself because you cannot act as a human being and do these things."

During World War I, the German threat was depicted on a poster as a mad marauding gorilla with a bloody club carrying a wailing female victim. Notice the words the gorilla is stepping on in the poster.

Dehumanizing the enemy is the practice of empires. They must relegate far away people to the status of not worthy of life because the empires army does not have an emotional connection with people they do not know or are not threatened by. We sailed across the Atlantic ocean to Europe to fight their wars twice so we had to demonize the German people two times. In Paul Craig Roberts book, *Empire of lies*, we find that "World War 2 began when the Churchill (English) government and the French declared war on Germany. Hitler's restoration of Germany's original national boundaries was misrepresented in the British and US press as 'German aggression.' This fake news story of German aggression was used to build the case that Germany, (which in truth was merely recovering its national territory taken from them by the Allies after WW1, and rescuing German people from persecution in Czechoslovakia and Poland) was an aggressor with world conquest as its goal. Hitler stated many times that he did not want, or intend, war with Britain and France and only intended to recover the lost German populations stolen from Germany by the unjust Versailles Treaty. This author understands the love affair America has with Hitlerizing any foreign leader America wants to overthrow for spoil and has been a personal witness to it as it has been played out by our Government and media over the decades. Sometimes "real history" needs to be considered and understood over the U.S. Empires conquests as the mainstream media whips up the American people into yet another frenzy of war hysteria.

In that same World War 2, American politicians interested in dragging the country into another European war knew the American people were against marching off to another quagmire across the Atlantic, so they had to bait Japan into attacking our Naval base in Pearl Harbor and then demonize them for taking the bait. With over 2400 U.S. Navy personnel assuming room temperature, Americans looked across the ocean and war was on and today we still celebrate December 7, as National Pearl Harbor Remembrance Day.

Taking a few steps further back in history in January 1898, the **battleship** *U.S.S. Maine* was sent to Havana, Cuba, during their war for independence from Spain to safeguard American interests there, although the Secretary of the Navy, John D. Long, insisted that it was only making a friendly call. A mysterious explosion destroyed the *Maine* on February 15, 1898, while in the Havana Harbor. Although the cause of the explosion was "said to be" unknown, the misguided American public soon became consumed with "war fever," blaming the Spanish in Cuba for the attack. But according to John E. Fahey, Historian, of the United States Naval History and Heritage Command, "the available physical and historical evidence overwhelmingly indicated the *Maine* was destroyed by an accident inside the ship." But with 268 U.S. Sailors dead, Remember the Maine!, became the battle cry to dehumanize the Spanish for this explosion on our ship.

Leaping forward in history the **"Gulf of Tonkin" incident** was an international confrontation that led to the United States war with Vietnam. It involved both a proven confrontation on August 2, 1964, carried out by North Vietnamese forces in response to U.S. covert operations in the coastal region of the gulf and a second, "claimed confrontation" on August 4, 1964, between ships of North Vietnam and the United States in the waters of the Gulf of Tonkin. Originally American claims blamed North Vietnam for both attacks. Later investigations revealed that the second attack never happened. The outcome of these two questionable confrontations was the passage by the U.S. Congress of the: **Gulf of Tonkin Resolution**, which granted U.S. President Lyndon B. Johnson the authority to assist any Southeast Asian country whose government was considered to be jeopardized by "communist aggression." The resolution served as Johnson's legal justification for deploying U.S. conventional forces and the commencement of open warfare against North Vietnam. Americas cost in the theater of Vietnam for a U.S. provoked incident and a non incident was over 58,000 dead,

And then it was in the summer of 1990, concerns were growing that **Iraqi President, Saddam Hussein**, who was massing troops near the border with Kuwait, was preparing an all-out invasion. U.S. Ambassador to Iraq, April Glaspie met with Saddam Hussein on July 25, 1990 to convey the United States' position. *The New York Times* on September 23, 1990 quotes Glaspie as saying, "We have no opinion on the Arab-Arab conflicts, like your border disagreement with Kuwait." It has been said by some that ambassador Glaspie who had a phone and the number of the White House was used to bait Saddam into attacking Kuwait. Historically Kuwait was actually part of Iraq until the British helped the locals carve it up and out of Iraq. So with the U.S. News belching out stories of Iraqi troops turning off baby incubators in Kuwait, America was once again whipped up into a war frenzy.

Then there was **Clinton and his bombing campaign of Serbia** in 1999 for the reason that the Serbians would not let the Albanians from neighboring Albania walk off with their historical city Kosovo. After the U.S. media Hitlerizing President Slobodan Milosevic of Yugoslavia, America freed the city from its rightful owners and summarily gave it to the people of Albania.

So now comes **911 in 2001**, with planes flying into New York buildings and watching the Twin Towers fall down exactly in their buildings foot print. During that same event a plane hit the Pentagon and one fell down in Pennsylvania. But many forget building 7 just across the street from the Towers that fell down all by itself and also in its exact building foot print seven hours later. Strange how New York buildings can do that. With over 3000 dead America was ready to be told who did this and blood was on their minds. So always ready to answer the call for war the U.S. Gov't, assisted by the mainstream media pulled an Osama Bin Laden out of their hat and pointed to Afghanistan. Never mind that he was reported to have died years ago.

We needed a boogie man and he fit the bill. So off to Afghanistan to start the forever war on terror. After 20 years of so called war in that country we finally up and left in 2021 and made sure the Ghani's were paid by leaving them 95 billion dollars of Americas military hardware and pallets of cash for their troubles.

Don't forget the **second invasion of Iraq in 2003** during our perpetual war on terror. It was George Bush the Junior, who claimed Saddam (or the Middle Eastern Hitler) was ramping up his nuclear arsenal by the purchase of 500 tons of yellow cake uranium powder purchased from Niger, which could be enriched and used in nuclear weapons. So with the Afghanistan war already in play, America's elites needed yet another engagement to continue their quest for power, but for mainstream America the war was revenge for our buildings just falling down like a perfect stack of pancakes.

And yet today the American people are once again asked to believe that Russia not only got Trump elected in 2016 but are now terrorizing the Ukrainian people. If you get your opinions of this war from the mainstream news then it can be said that you as an American have not learned nothing from history and still have no clue on how this country operates. For those who remember it was U.S. Secretary of State James Baker's famous "not one inch eastward" assurance about NATO expansion in his meeting with Soviet leader Mikhail Gorbachev on February 9, 1990, that was part of a cascade of assurances about Soviet security given by Western leaders to Gorbachev and other Soviet officials throughout the process of the German reunification of the East and West in 1990. There were 16 NATO signatory countries at the time Mr. "not one inch" shot his mouth off. Today there are 31 NATO countries and four that border Russia. So who broke that treaty? And now Ukraine which also borders Russia is now requesting NATO membership. Russia knows if that country becomes a member they will acquire NATO missile defense systems that can hit Moscow in 5 minutes. Seems America would not allow

Russia to put missiles on Cuban soil in 1962 so why would we expect Russia to let NATO put missile systems on their door step. If one is interested in what is really going on in Ukraine I would suggest turning off your idiot box and checking out the internet sites: https://halturnerradioshow.com/index.php/en and https://www.naturalnews.com/Index.html. Canadian Prepper and Scott Ritter on Youtube

Now if there ever was a legitimate reason for war as in an invasion of our country by a foreign power there would be no need to demonize anyone. The emotion would be assured as our army would come to the defense of their homeland. But this is not the way of empires. Having to create events leading to wars to accomplish goals not fully understood by the ones that have to do all the bleeding IS the way of empires. The empire uses a complicit media to demonize the chosen boogie man for their created event and the American people are expected to show their patriotism by killing a whole lot of people they never met, but not all of them. Because once the goal of war has been accomplished the U.S. Gov't begins the process of moving a large segment of the targeted country's residents back here so we can financially take care of them. Thus continuing the ongoing process of America's quest for yet more multiculturalism by adding more races of people which gives us more religions, more conflicting histories, multiple languages, and many customs not fully understood by this host country. All these multi-cultures all competing for resources within the borders of America has caused our elites to come up with a pacifying slogan for the masses of fly-over country: Diversity is our strength!

It was on February 20, 2010, when *CNB News*, reported that just before Christmas, that five soldiers who were part of the Arab translation program at Fort Jackson, SC, were investigated after they allegedly were overheard discussing plans to poison food at the base. Army Criminal Investigation Division spokesman Christopher Gray further revealed to CNB reporter Erick Stakelbaeck, that the "Fort Jackson Five" were part of a small unit at the base called 09 Lima, a part of the Civilian Skills Program, which welcomes into the military non-U.S. Citizens who speak Arabic. One of the program's directors, Lt. Col. Frank Deminth, explains that these recruits are then placed into an expedited citizenship program, "once they serve one day of honorable active duty."

Rose colored glasses cannot begin to explain the dangerous ignorance of the people who are in charge of protecting this country's freedom. Multiculturalism has been historically proven to be unstable at best, but when mixed with the military it has the ability to be devastating to all involved.

TRUE MULTICULTURAL NATIONS DO NOT EXCLUDE

For the White Southerner, egalitarianism seems to stop right there on the Mason-Dixon Line in this country. With all the cultures we have to deal with in America we are told we have no room for one of its oldest. It seems just about every country needs a local demon to blame for its ills. Iraq has those pesky Kurds, Mexico has the Zapatistas, and historical Germany had the Jews. Here in America we have chosen the region of the South to carry the banner of the great unwashed guilty. The White South that is. Nowhere in America will you find a more vilified people. From insulting the way they talk, their "perceived" dental hygiene, to their historic battle flag. There is nothing easier and more acceptable than crapping on those White Southerners. So how can a true multicultural country with an open door policy to all peoples of the world including known terrorists truly be multicultural if they reject one of their own founding cultures? I remember years ago working for a firm in Los Angeles having just announced I was North Carolina bound. Kind of going home for me since I can claim Southern blood. After my announcement some co-workers I barely even talked to before were coming up to me with a smirk or a sneer on their faces saying things like, "oh, you're going to that place with all those KKKers." Or comments like, "I remember going through Tennessee, geez don't those people ever see a dentist?" The confidence these Californians had with insulting the South was not astonishing but really typical. The national acceptance of insulting the South is so deeply ingrained in American society that Hollywood has made great money off it. For example, years ago watching a film about some rock band helps to hammer this point in. The band wasn't even a southern rock band but when the rape scene came on guess what was pinned to the wall framing the crime? The Rebel flag, the Stars and Bars, aka the St. Andrews cross flag. How many times have we seen the South portrayed in the movies as backward, stupid, and racist?

The South has been taking it on the chin since 1861 for several reasons. First and how can anyone ever forget the so called and incorrectly titled "Civil War" claimed by the winners to be fought over slavery? The next sin was the birthing of that group called the KKK. Following that crew the next violation was the role the South played in the 1960's Civil Rights Movement. The last sin was acquiring the unique regional title of: The Bible Belt. How dare those Bible thumping racists continue their backward practice of promoting that unprogressive, intolerant, religion called Christianity! Yes, to America the sins of the South are many and probably demographically unfixable to the Northern standard of acceptability. So lets examine these sins pinned onto the South. Lets see what floats and what don't.

~ Taxes, Secession, and Slavery, Who did it first? ~

The first sin: Having the audacity to want to secede from the mother country brought on an historical event called - The Civil War, which has caused the commitment of vast resources by the winners of that conflict to re-write its history as they wish it to be. After all, those Southerners started the Civil War by not freeing their slaves didn't they? Now we cannot compare those revolutionary war secessionist heroes to what those Southerners did because it's just not the same thing right? Just because those Revolutionary Patriots wanted to secede from their mother country Britain with their slaves in tow because of taxes, in Ameri-think it cannot be compared to 85 years later when the South wanted to secede from their mother country with their slaves in tow for basically the same reason of taxes. Ah, says the historically ignorant of the world. The big difference here is that the Civil War was not fought over taxes but over slavery. My daddy told me that, my school teacher said it, and the cartoon I watched when I was 7 agreed with them both. Case closed, matter settled, time to move on. Well can we look at this chunk of history with more of a slant towards reality?

First, the South was not fighting the North for governing dominance over this country called America just as the Revolutionary Patriots were not fighting to rule Britain. Before the hostilities broke out, the South announced to the North their decision to peacefully secede from the Union. Got it? *Peacefully secede* from the UNION. They informed the North that they would assume their regional fare share of the country's current debt and also would pay the Federal government for its monetary investment in Federal buildings and infrastructure in the South. What this proves is the South did not want to take over the North and rule it. Tossing aside the silly watered down history your teacher threw at you as a toddler, the real reason for Southern secession was that the South was being economically bled dry by the North with the help of the passage of that infamous tariff in 1828 called, "The Tariff of Abominations" by its Southern detractors because of the effects it had on the Souths antebellum economy. It was imposed on the South by the Northern majority in Congress to benefit the Northern industrial interest by subsidizing their production through high prices and public works. But it had the effect of forcing the agrarian South to pay more for manufactured goods from the industrial North and thus disproportionately taxing it to support the U.S. Central Government. Thirty years later with the South paying 87% of the Federal tariff revenue, it became impossible for the two regions to be governed equally. Mr. Lincoln was the leading advocate of the day with regards to this infamous tariff, so when the dude with the stove top hat got elected in 1860, the South fearing economic ruin seceded.

It was in January of 1861 when the South officially seceded lead by the State of South Carolina and ten more states followed. These eleven Southern States formed the Confederate States of America, or the CSA. It was in April of that same year that President Lincoln decided to send supplies to (Federal) Fort Sumter in South Carolina. Fort Sumter was a customs house. Lincoln put South Carolina on notice in advance of his intentions to resupply Fort Sumter in (some say) a so called attempt to avoid hostilities, while (others say) to force the secession issue militarily. I cannot for the life of me think that if you let someone know you are going to resupply a military fort in their back yard that they would think it was an attempt to avoid any type of hostility but that's just me right? But South Carolina however smelled a rat and on April 12, 1861, the so called Civil War began with shots fired on the fort. So up to this point can anyone say that the hostilities at Fort Sumter were caused by the North trying to end slavery in the South? Does resupplying a fort that was a customs house sound like a tax issue or a slave issue? The record is clear that Lincoln, that great emancipator, was trying to keep the issue of slavery out of the war. Why? Because he feared it would weaken the northern war effort. He knew at that time the Northern troops would fight to save the Union but they would not fight to free the slaves. How do we know this? It seems this war President needed the support of the five Northern border "slave" states that had not left the Union. Delaware, Kentucky, Maryland, Missouri, and his newly carved out unconstitutional state of West Virginia. The reason slavery was not the cause of the war was made even clearer by Lincoln himself in a letter he wrote on August 22, 1862, in response to an editorial by Horace Greeley of the *New York Tribune* which urged complete abolition. Lincoln wrote in response: "my paramount object in this struggle is to save the Union, and is not either to save or destroy slavery. If I could save the Union without freeing any slave I would do it." Any questions? So today as the Indians and Italians fight over Columbus's navigating skills, Northerners and Blacks still faint over the great non-emancipator, Lincoln. To add a little weight to this issue that the so called Civil War was NOT fought over slavery we have a document that just won't go away. Two days before Lincoln's inauguration as the 16th president, Congress, consisting of only the northern states, passed overwhelmingly on March 2, 1861, the Corwin Amendment that gave constitutional protection to slavery. Lincoln endorsed the amendment in his inaugural address saying, "I have no objection to its being made express and irrevocable." Quite clearly, the North was not prepared to go to war to end slavery when on the very eve of war the US Congress and incoming president were in the process of making it unconstitutional to abolish slavery. But as they say, a funny thing happened on the way to the forum. By the second year of the war things were not going as planned. Those pesky Southerners were actually making a fight of it and even winning. A new issue was needed to keep the war spirit up in the North. So instead of a white rabbit, Lincoln decided it was time to pull a Black slave out of his hat. In January 1863 the guy with the big hat "now" told the world that the war was about slavery and announced his much heralded, although kind of late, Emancipation Proclamation. By God this man had decided it was time to free the slaves in America! Well....not all slaves mind you, but most certainly the ones living in those Rebel States for sure. It seems the great one left out those five Northern border slave states of his proclamation thus exempting them from freeing their slaves, causing some to believe that this proclamations real purpose was to cause a slave uprising in the South to help the war effort. So with his new proclamation of announcing that the slaves in another country (he was not in charge of) are now free, and leaving slavery still intact in the Northern border states (of which he was in charge of) the war took a new turn. In fact that Yankee hero and soon to be President, Union General Ulysses S. Grant was not at all impressed or economically impacted by this emancipation having slaves himself (as did other Yankee Generals) who only after the war freed their slaves once the 13th amendment passed in December of 1865. When asked why he did not free his slaves earlier Grant replied, "good help is hard to come by these days."

But we as American citizens have learned we must always cling to the myth that Lincoln fought the so-called Civil War over slavery. So yes its true. Winners of wars do re-write history. To sum it all up.

- The war started in 1861.
- The Emancipation Proclamation of 1863 was enacted to free the slaves only in the Confederate South.
- This proclamation to free the slaves in the Confederate States exempted the five Northern border slave states.
- The proclamation also didn't apply to the Yankee slave owning generals during the war.

So are there any laws enacted in this country to prevent secession or make it illegal for its citizens to pursue secession? No, in fact there is this one historical U.S. Document that actually gives the act of secession the legal green light. Not wanting to be a document name dropper or anything but we might want to look at the first official document of this nation called, "The Declaration of Independence" to see what this country's founders view on the act of secession truly was. You don't have to look very far. It's right there in the second paragraph.

> *Governments are instituted among Men, deriving their just powers from the consent of the governed, --That whenever any Form of Government becomes destructive of these ends, it is the Right of the People to alter or to abolish it, and to institute new Government, laying its foundation on such principles and organizing its powers in such form, as to them shall seem most likely to effect their Safety and Happiness.*

Now the next question that begs for an answer is: Was the Declaration of Independence a "good for one time only" document?

Does this Declaration have any relevance or current meaning to the people of this country today? Does it demand a place of honor in the annals of America or should it be discarded to the outdated and no longer applicable pile? I would guess that the majority of people in this country actually believe those words written in the Declaration are as honorable today as they were when the men wrote them back then. Now this document doesn't say anywhere that *"the right of the people to alter or abolish it and institute a new government"* was just meant for the people who fought the Revolutionary War right? When defining rights, the Declaration specifically says, *"the right of the people"* NOT "the right of those people fighting the Revolutionary War, correct? Did they write in this document that future generations "could not" or even "should not" follow the founders footsteps in future secessions? No. Can we assume that the founders wrote this section in the Declaration because they believed in the act of secession and wanted their following ancestors to understand what they did and why they believed they were within their rights to secede? So who really believed that the founding American document called The Declaration of Independence was legitimate and legal as it pertained to the War to prevent the legal secession of the South? The South we can determine understood the founders true intent of America's founding document and was legally following in the founders footsteps when it seceded. The North obviously did not possess the understanding of what it means to belong to a union created by consenting States because how can any rational thinking individual come to the conclusion that the original consenting Colonial States would have even considered joining the Union if they knew they would be attacked if they desired to leave at a later date? Let us not forget before there was a United States there were neighboring Colonial States that were not united. The word is "choice" folks. This Union of States called "The United States" was originally formed by the individual States choice of volunteering to join together and not by coercion. We cannot make the claim that this nation is held together today by volunteering States anymore can we? In fact the individual States today and since 1861 are now bound together by the threat of war. I can say with much confidence that this is not what the founders had in mind when they formed this more perfect union. As Albert Bledsoe, a Southern writer of that time said, "the denial to a people of the right to self determination was bad enough, but the martyrdom of leaders captured after an abortive struggle for independence marked the end of the spirit in which the American government had been conceived."

A clear case can be made for claiming that the so called Civil War was not really a Civil War at all in its true sense. What that war can be correctly defined as is "a war of Northern aggression to prevent Southern Independence." The real definition of a Civil War is two entities fighting for dominance over a common geographical area. Again, same as the historic Revolutionaries of America did not want to rule England, neither did the South want to rule the North. Indeed these first secessionists with slaves in tow who fought America's war for independence are idolized today as heroes by this nation. But a mere 85 years later we find the South being demonized for trying to do exactly the same thing for basically the same reason. From an historical perspective this is an odd way to look at the history of this nation with regards to the issue of secession. This country called America was founded on secession, celebrates secession every Fourth of July, and idolizes its original secessionists. But as citizens in Ameri-think, we are told that our government is selective when deciding who can or cannot secede in this country. We are told we cannot apply those same historical principles to the South's quest for freedom as we can to the original founders quest for freedom. We are told to ignore the secession validating words in this countrys founding document because even though it doesn't say it, those words must have been only relevant during one time period only.

So today as this President called Abe is celebrated as the great emancipator, the South continues to be demonized over secession and slavery and we, the citizens of America, are informed by our government, our schools, and the media, that we must never lift up that American history rug to see where all those inconvenient truths are hidden. Sorry Al, it just seems to fit here.

~ The KKK and other assorted nasty's ~

Yes, everybody's favorite racial target in America is none other than the KKK, or the Ku Klux Klan. The **second sin** of the South. This organization was formed in Pulaski Tennessee, during the era of Reconstruction by six former Confederate officers including the famous Calvary General, Nathan Bedford Forest being one of them. It started out as a prankish social club but its later activities were soon directed at the Northern Reconstruction government and their leaders both Black and White in defense of the Southern people. Associated with activities such as cross burning, white sheets, and some notable lynchings, this group was eventually put on the socially undesirable map. But again look at the times during Reconstruction. There is this thing called "cause and effect." With Union soldiers still strong arming the South after the war, carpetbaggers trying to economically bleed it dry, and Black and White Northern leaders systematically tearing down what was left of the White Antebellum South, it was only a matter of time before something was going to give.

The original KKK disbanded in the early 1870's around the time Reconstruction ended but was revived again around 1915 in opposition mainly to Catholic and Jewish immigration to the U.S. The second revival of this group went nationwide especially in the Midwest. Get it? Midwest or geographically speaking – Yankville. So now one of the main causes of the national resurrection of the KKK was unwanted immigration. Seems people from both sides of the Mason-Dixon even back then were not happy with their governments never ending love affair with bombing its citizens with immigrants. In the North the Klan rose to prominence especially in the state of Indiana in their politics and society after World War I. The group was made up of native born White protestants of all income and social levels. Indiana's Klan organization reached its peak of power in the following years when it had 250,000 members, an estimated 30% of that States native born White men. By 1925, over half the elected members of the Indiana General Assembly, the Governor of Indiana, and many other high ranking officials in local and state government were members of the Klan. That states politicians also learned they needed the Klan endorsement to win office. It looks to me like the sin of the South spread North and became a national sin.

It is estimated today that there are 190 active KKK groups with between 5000 and 8000 Klan members in the U.S. But listening to the media you would think the KKK was not only the most powerful hate group active in America but really the only hate group in America. But go west and you'll find another group called the Aryan Nations that was originally located near Hayden Lake, Idaho. The Aryan Nations is one of the country's best known enclaves of anti-semitism and White nationalism. While originally founded as a Christian Identity post, the organization incorporated neo-Nazi themes. It's founder and longtime leader Richard Butler openly adulated Hitler. Since many of its members belonged to other White supremacist groups, it was no surprise that the Aryan Nations compound at Hayden Lake had served as one of the central meeting points of the far right. Currently the Aryan Nations are reported to have groups in Oregon, Ohio, and Pennsylvania.

Stepping out of the White racial realm of such groups you will find a fertile field of groups who hate but are conveniently not always labeled as hate groups. Surely after listening to the founder and leader of the Nation of Islam one would come away with the notion that *Louis Farrakhan* is more than unimpressed with the White people he calls – blue eyed devils. Just as surely he has been known to blame those same blue eyed devils for all the ills of the Black man. He has been reported to have said, "*White people are potential humans.*" We all know if a White person said Blacks were potential humans, that every White, Black, Purple, and Green organization in America would be calling for social justice and economic retribution for the next 300 years. Other famous quotes by our friend are just as illuminating. On the Jewish people he is quoted saying: *"you are wicked deceivers of the American people. You have sucked their blood,"* And then there was this, *"my god will wipe this country (America) from the face of the earth."* In August of 2015 *Worldnetdaily* reported, "preaching directly from the Quran before a packed Baptist church, the Nation of Islam leader Louis Farrakhan told his adoring audience that, *"violent retaliation is the only way for American Blacks to rise up and overthrow their White oppressors."* So can you call Louis Farrakhan and the Nation of Islam racists or not?

Are there other Black hate groups in America? You wouldn't come to that conclusion if you got your news from the Lamestream media. But as always one must develop that practice of lifting up the corner of the media rug to see where the real news is hiding. *Professor Walter Williams* (a Black man) in his 1999 article titled: An ugly conspiracy of silence, tells us: "That we Americans all readily condemn highly publicized racial violence and rightly so. However there's little notice and condemnation of interracial crimes when Whites are the victims. Since 1972 the U.S. Dept. of Justice has conducted a National Crime Victimization Survey (NCVS). One category is interracial crimes. It's publication in 1997, Criminal Victimization in the U.S. Reports on the data collected and in 90% of racial crime cases, a White was the victim and a Black was the perpetrator. If the facts were the other way around would not everybody from the New York Times, President Clinton, NAACP, Jesse Jackson, and the Congressional Black Caucus, be shouting about it and demanding something be done? Mr. Williams goes on to say that, "Multi-ethnic Societies are inherently unstable, and how we handle matters of interracial crime is just one of the ways that we're contributing to that instability."

So as this Black Professor has just informed us, Whites are the victims and Blacks are the perpetrators of 90% of racial crimes in

America involving these two races. Could you say there is a racial hatred in the Black American population? It is reported that the violent black gang "the Crips" have an estimated 30,000 to 35,000 members while the black gang "the Bloods" have 15,000 to 20,000 members. Do you think these combined 50,000 gang members can cause more crime and fear than around 7000 KKKers? You wouldn't know by listening to the TV news. Hold on you may say. These gangs are just criminals and not racists. Well lets test that theory. If you are a pale face then why don't you take an evening stroll in one of their gang controlled territories.

In Denver back in 2009, Black gangs roaming downtown often vented their hatred for White victims before assaulting and robbing them during an ongoing four month crime wave. One unidentified suspect told police that members of his gang earn status by beating up White dudes. Sounds like a racist group to me.

Has anyone ever thought of why the American has this bizarre kind of bipolar view of racist crime? Ask yourself why your mind would go into automatic over-drive of fearing dangerous nation threatening racism if an organized White group attacked Blacks. Then ask why your mind would go on automatic under-drive if an organized Black group attacked Whites, as you now view these crimes as non-important isolated events. I, for one fully understand how you acquired that bipolar view of racial crime Mr. Socially Engineered American. So can I claim to have uncovered a conspiracy in the media that exhibits a double standard in America today with regards to labeling who is a racist? As Hollywood, the Government, the Media, and our Schools, commit serious time and resources warning us of the evils of White racism, shouldn't they be expanding their definition to include all groups that hate and not just their favorite target the KKK?

~ Hippie's, Drugs, Braless Women, and those Uppity N-words ~

The **third sin** of the South was finding itself right in the cross hairs of the Civil Rights Movement which piggy backed in on the culture war of the 1960's. Those who were there during the sixties know how it was. Those who were not still know how it was, albeit through the liberal slanted versions of those countless PBS government documentaries, Hollywood movies, and watered down school room lessons, all designed to make one segment of our population look evil, one to look oppressed, and a few to look heroic.

The 1964 Civil Rights Act was signed by one of our favorites, President Lyndon B. Johnson. Yes, our favorite busy body was at it again. This act was basically a left hook to the South which forced racial integration, but not only to the South but to the nation as a whole. The act basically was the endcap follow up of a ten years earlier situation the Government decided to stir up. That year was 1954 when the U.S. Supreme Court decision in *Brown v. Board of Education,* declared racial segregation in public schools unconstitutional. The process of integrating public schools met fierce resistance in the South where segregation laws took hold after the Civil War and the Reconstruction era. A backlash of resistance and violence ensued. Even members of Congress refused to abide by the decision and in 1956 over a hundred congressmen signed the *Southern Manifesto*, promising to use all legal means to undermine and reverse the Court's ruling. The impact of the ruling in both the North and the South was limited because Whites and Blacks tended to live in separate communities. The governments struggle to desegregate the schools received the push it needed ten years later from the Blacks Civil Rights Movement, whose goal was to dismantle legal segregation in all public places. The movements efforts struck gold in Congress when the Civil Rights Act of 1964 was passed. The sweeping legislation signaled the end of the segregation of public accommodations. The impact of this Act was the injection of both legislative and executive branches joining the judiciary to promote racial integration. In addition the Act authorized the federal government to cut off funding if Southern school districts did not comply and also bring lawsuits against school officials who resisted.

In 1968, the Warren Court in *Green v. County School Board of New Kent County,* rejected a freedom of choice plan. The Court ordered the county to desegregate immediately and eliminate racial discrimination. Then in 1971, the Burger Court in *Swann v. Charlotte-Mecklenburg Board of Education,* ruled that the school district must achieve racial balance even if it meant redrawing school boundaries and including the use of "busing" as a legal tool. "Busing" is taking kids out of their neighborhood schools and busing them to other parts of town schools to force racial integration. The impact of the *Green* and *Swann* rulings served to end all remnants of *de jure* segregation in the South.

I am not going to go back in history and go point for point here because I think the main issue of Civil Rights for the most part has been settled. Who can really argue the point that the negro population was not discriminated against in certain ways back then in both the South and the North? Who can tell us today that a person named Rosa Parks should have given up her seat on that bus to a White man just because she was Black? Back then the Whites would sometimes call a Black who either smarted off or were standing up for their equal rights, the uppity N-word. So referencing the Rosa Parks situation we can all understand that her point of reference was coming from the latter of this uppity N-word statement and she was standing up for her equal rights. So change did come to the South and like all social changes within societies it came with a struggle. But like all issues there are two sides. So just maybe for once we'll take a look at the other side. The Southern side that is.

In 1964 the South was one hundred years away from a war that had devastated her cities and around 85 years out of another disaster called Reconstruction. After losing the war in 1865, having suffered, bled, and died, trying to get out of the Union, the South not only found herself back in it, but also being dragged into a new postwar police action that would curse the South for 12 years. The goal of the Northern enforced Reconstruction was not only to punish the South but to revolutionize Southern Society. One of the mandates of Reconstruction was to disenfranchise all former military and civil officers of the Confederacy and all those who owned property worth $20,000 or more, and make their estates liable for confiscation. The obvious intent of this program was to seize political control in the South from the old gentleman planter aristocracy. The emotional effects of this political reconstruction haunted the South for decades afterwards.

With still vivid memories of a pyromaniac Union General named William T. Sherman, the pleasure of being over-lorded by the North for more than a decade under the banner of Reconstruction was for some a little more than they could take. Who's Sherman some might say? Why he is the guy who had a fetish for bombing and burning women and children out of their homes and is on record saying, "there is a class of people (Southerners) men, women, and children, who must be killed or banished before you can hope for peace and order." One of Lincolns favorite generals. To pour a little oil on that fire, over two hundred Negroes were placed in political office during Reconstruction in the defeated South as a result of Northern Republican efforts to "refashion" the Southern government and to compensate for centuries of slavery. Now this compensation was for Southern Slavery only mind you, no compensation for Northern slavery needed. Funny isn't it that is was reported that only two Blacks are known to have held public office in the North during the Civil War era. How bad was Reconstruction? It was the South's most famous General and resident, Robert E. Lee himself who said, "if I had foreseen the ravages of Reconstruction I would have not surrendered but instead died with my men right there at Appomattox." So is it really far-fetched that the White Southerner would hold some level of resentment for these reasons listed below?

- Being subjected to ruinous taxes by the North for 30 years before the Civil War.
- Being attacked by the North for basically following in the footsteps of the founders documented validation of the peoples right to secede in the Declaration of Independence.
- Having been made the victim of a new kind of war invented by the Northern government called "Total War" which advocated and prosecuted the wholesale bombing and burning of much of the civilian infrastructure in the South and any women and children who were unfortunate enough to be in it.
- After losing the war then having to be subjected to 12 years of social and economic destruction by way of Northern enforced Reconstruction.

Now zoom forward some ninety years and here comes yet another change the South did not ask for and that change had the face of a man called Martin Luther King. Now it is known that the Reverend was no beacon of morality. Him being a preacher and to quote one of his captains, Ralph David Abernethy in his book, *And the walls came tumbling down*, "Martin had an eye for the women that led to an adulterous sex life." To add to those infidelities there were reported at that time various allegations of the Reverends serious connections with some seditious Communists of that day. But that being said the South was on her own on this one too! In the 1960's it was Black vs. White in the South. The media and the Government chose their side and once again the South took it on the chin. With water hoses and Police German Shepards on one side and unarmed protesters on the other, it wasn't hard for the media to crown the winner.

But it seems what the Blacks were calling equal rights the Whites were calling desegregation. Was it wrong for the Black population of that time period to want their equal rights? No thinking person can argue against that point. Was it wrong for the White South to want to be left alone and live their lives the way they chose, all be it separate?

Your busy body liberal elites will argue that point. But take another look back at that famous Declaration of Independence and even the Southerner is now getting confused. What happened to that famous American theme?

> *....We hold these truths to be self evident that all men are created equal, that they are endowed by their creator with certain unalienable Rights that among these are life, liberty, and the pursuit of happiness.*

SIDE NOTE: To clear up the *all men are created equal*, issue there is in Ameri-think the idea that Blacks were counted as 3/5ths of a person in the Constitution. The site: *BlackPast.org*, explains it away. "Often misinterpreted to mean that African Americans as individuals are considered 3/5ths of a person or that they are 3/5ths of a citizen of the U.S., the 3/5ths clause (Article 1, Section 2, of the U.S. Constitution of 1787) in fact declared that for the purposes of representation in Congress, enslaved Blacks in a State would be counted as 3/5ths of the number of White inhabitants of that State." Since as a child I saw a cartoon on this constitutional subject displaying a black individual with 3/5ths of a body, I just thought I would get that one out of the way first.

Now back to the issue at hand. Look again at the *"endowed by their Creator with certain unalienable rights to pursue life liberty and happiness"* line in the Declaration. According to the Founders writing here these rights listed in this document were not government authorized but given to us by God. If it is written that the Founders understood that God had given us rights such as "Life Liberty and the Pursuit of Happiness" then it stands to reason that man cannot take these same rights away because according to the Founders, man did not give us these rights in the first place. It says we as Americans received those rights from a higher source. So how far of a stretch is it to say if the Southern Whites wanted to exercise their God given rights to pursue their idea of happiness by living separate from Blacks or any other race for that matter, what legal grounds could the U.S. Government stand on to deny these God given rights? Is not the Declaration of Independence America's first legal document or not? Looking back it seems like Uncle Sam was the one breaking the countrys own laws here by forcing racial desegregation in the South doesn't it?

Nevertheless after the Civil Rights struggle the South became the Liberal elites favorite whipping boy in this country and that practice continues to this day. So as with all shoves there comes a push, a push back that is. With a developing historical grievance of their own, a few pro-secession movements have turned up in the South and are calling for a new look at it. But looking back at the turbulent sixties we can determine that: The hippies were successful in ushering in the counter culture with a more open and general acceptance of drugs and sex; the woman moved out of the house and into the workforce; and the American Negro won his desegregation war against the South and really the country as a whole.

~ Bible thumpers and other politically incorrect things ~

The **fourth sin** of the South is that they happen to be the only region in the world that can claim the distinct title of: The Bible Belt. Southerners on balance are proud of that label as well they should be. But in a multicultural world not all Americans view that title with envy. Is not Christianity today now viewed as an intolerant religion? Funny how the non-Christians insist on removing the crosses and religious monuments from public view thus exhibiting some of that famous Liberal intolerance we in this country have become accustomed to experiencing over the years. Equally as funny though, as the body count ratchets up under the religion of Islam we are not hearing a lot about that kind of intolerance from our Government and media are we? It's just that cross bearing crew that receives most of the negative press in America. But isn't it strange how since as far back as one can remember, Jews and people of color have migrated en masse to these so called intolerant historic White Christian nations of this world in search of a better life. Can you think of a time in history when it was the White Christian doing the same en masse for the same reason? Not exactly.

The main reason for that is "usually" when the White Christian historically migrated en masse to another territory, by God he marched in, subdued the locals, set up shop, formed his own government, and many times Christianized the infidels. But moving forward to today a good part of the indigenous world is grateful for the Christian coming to their countries, feeding them, providing medical supplies and treatment, and most importantly bringing the knowledge of Christ with them. The Christian missionary business is booming today and when those missionaries from America are traveling to 3rd world countries to build houses for the poor, last I heard they were getting asked to come back. But isn't it odd that in the country where these missionaries come from we are witnessing a rise in anti-Christian sentiment within the media and the Government? This anti-Christian sentiment produces actions such as the removal of religious symbols and monuments from public view, threatening students who pray in school, to a full blown war declared on Christian holidays. Since nowhere in America is the Christian religion more promoted and dominant than in the South, the sin of being saddled with the title of: The Bible Belt, receives full regional condemnation in many forms by many individuals, institutions, and even some races as well. You would think America would be grateful for the good will and positive influence our Christian ambassadors bring to the world. But as Political and corporate America disparages the exportation of Christian good will, it concentrates its energy on other world exports such as the Arms trade and Porn exploitation. Talk about a strange paradox. As America tightens the screws on in-country gun sales to its citizens, the

American defense industry is the undisputed champion of the global arms market. In 2014 the U.S. Exported over $36.2 billion in weaponry, accounting for over 60% of the total arms sold worldwide according to a report by the *Congressional Research Service*. Trailing the U.S. in weapons receipts was Russia with $10.2 billion in sales in 2014. *The Blaze* on June 13, 2013 reported that America is also the leading exporter of Porn. A full 60% of the worlds porn sites come from that anti-Bible Belt country and again not a close second to be found. So as America sexualizes the world and then sells it enough military ordinance to blow themselves off the map can we ask ourselves the simple question: What is so bad about feeding the worlds poor, caring for their sick, and building them houses, while enriching their lives with Christ? The key to Ameri-think is to not think too hard.

So there you have it and there it is. The four sins of the South. From the Civil War to Civil Rights, the South has had to endure more than its fair share of social struggles. As Confederate monuments are brought down, southern streets renamed, battle flags banned, and the names of its heroes disappear from memory through institutionalized coercion, the Southerner knows one thing for sure: In this multicultural worshiping country called America, all new cultures are welcomed, but one of the main founding cultures is not. And that would be the most Christian one.

MULTICULTURALISM, THE ANTI-THESIS OF BLOOD AND SOIL

A culture in its historic and organic form is basically a people with a common blood, common symbols, common language, common history, common customs, values, and traditions, and a common religion. There's that "blood" word again. Just try to understand that this negative feeling that just came over some of you when you heard that word was socially engineered in you by the self appointed anointed through their media, the government, and those public schools. Your ancestors did not squirm at the mention of blood. They understood it. They instinctively knew a culture is basically a brotherhood. Your are either a part of it our you're not.

~ A Culture Defined ~

Envision if you can a blond haired person of Germanic origin wearing a traditional African skirt, a tribal headdress, and beating a drum. Not easy is it. Imagine a Black person wearing a Scottish kilt and playing the bagpipes. Seem odd? Imagine a Jew wearing either. Still having trouble? These symbols play an important role in connecting an individual to his culture. Symbols and traditions are some of the historic roots that give a person cultural stability in their lives. They help the individual understand who he is, where he came from, and what he generally thinks about certain things. Under the linguistic elements of culture imagine that same Black American wanting to learn to speak Irish Gaelic, or the same German wanting to learn the language of the African Hutu tribe. If his job doesn't require it, you can't imagine it. Is it possible for an Arab living in Scotland and a Scotsman to feel the same sense of pride if they both sing the song, "Scotland the Brave" the unofficial anthem of Scotland? I think you get the idea that I could fill half this chapter with similar comparisons exemplifying how unique cultural symbols and traditions apply to a certain type of racial or ethnic people under a common bloodline.

The reason that blood and culture are two words that cannot be separated is because it is the blood that creates the culture . It was those Zulu warriors that designed those colorful tribal headdresses and drums. Not one Italian was hired as a wardrobe consultant by the Zulu tribe to advise them on fashion. They did it on their own because it not only suited their unique needs but that is the way they wanted to do it. It was the people of Roman blood that invented central heating with no Chinese assistance. But didn't the Chinese invent gun powder? Who cannot be amazed at the castles in Europe or endlessly contemplate the glories of the Sphinx? Who cannot wonder at the amazing survival instincts of the Eskimos who are able to carve out an existence in one of the worlds most hostile environments? It was culture shaped by blood that created these wonders of the world.

Now lets take the next step. We know what a culture is but let us deal with the expression: Culture as a Nation. In Pat Buchanan's book: *State of Emergency,* I can think of no better example of finer writing on the subject than in the chapter called: What is a Nation?

> *"It is a passionate attachment to one's own country – its land, its people, its heroes, literature, traditions, culture, and customs. It is what enables a people to endure. Patriotism is the soul of a nation. It is what keeps a nation alive. When patriotism dies, the nation dies and begins to decompose. A nation is not*

defined by institutions but by language, religion, and high culture. A nation in a real sense is an extended family. A group of people who believe they are ancestrally related with a common set of values, customs, and a basic common view of their future."

Historically a people of common ancestry create a culture. Then these same people build on their cultures success which can eventually evolve into a nation. In the basic sense was it not the Irish who created the Ireland we know today? Was it not the Arabs who created Saudi Arabia? Now we can all go back in history and cite foreign conquests and racial migrations that changed various nations to varying degrees, especially when referencing Europe, but again I am talking about the Nation/State as defined in their basic sense. For example, when you go to Greece today you are going to see Greeks and experience Greek culture. Here are the three basic historical steps in the natural process of how a culture molds itself into a nation.

   a. A people of common blood, common origin, common language, common values and customs, and usually a common religion, create by needs and desires and by geographical default – a culture.

With the historical success of their thriving culture they take the next logical step and form a unique nation within defined borders recognizing official customs and a governing authority.

Once the people have established a Nation/State, their culture will take on a life of its own. It will become bigger than the individuals who created it and if respected, nurtured, and defended, it will serve as the governing authority of the peoples values and beliefs. It will also serve as a guide for raising and educating the young and it will become the light on the pathway to the peoples future.

The culture of a nation is kept secure and healthy by the respect and observance of the elders as they pass down through the generations the traditions such as the stories of the nations heroes, the accepted rules of conduct and courtship, to the holidays they celebrate. People living in a healthy culture have acquired the understanding that their culture is bigger and more important than the individual and that their rights come from the rules and traditions of their defined culture. That the survival of their people depends upon the unity of the individuals within their culture. To place their individual wants and desires above the health, unity, and destiny of their people and culture is divisive at least and damaging at most. To us an analogy: *A culture is like a car. If you take care of it, it will safely transport you in the future.*

Imagine a Mexican without Cinco de Mayo, or a Jew without Yom Kippur. These cultural traditions help define the very soul of a nation and its people. Think your culture is not important? Try waking up one morning in America knowing there will never be another Christmas or Easter holiday to celebrate. Try to envision your language suddenly being changed to another. Or maybe you wake up one morning and find out America has decided to adopt the Middle Eastern tradition of honor killings. (a judgment on Arab women) But also consider how one persons cultural endearment can be a cause for a yawn or even an offense to another person in the multicultural nation. If a Southerner sings the song Dixie affectionately reflecting back on his fond memories of the Old South, is the Cuban living in Miami going to eagerly join in? Can the American Hindu living in Charleston, South Carolina, consider the song Dixie to be an historic cultural value to him? Not hardly. But to take the situation further that same song could be viewed as offensive to say a person of Northern decent or even an African American as it may conjure up feelings such as a long dead relative or memories of ancestral slavery. What is a value to one culture can be of no value to another or even considered a negative value. This is why the social experiment of multiculturalism is, was, and will always be, not a true culture. Multiculturalism makes the egalitarian claim that all cultures are equal. But how can that be true when one persons cultural traditions and values can be in a constant state on continual conflict with another persons traditions and values? The conflicting ideologies of multiculturalism by its very existence "must" cause social friction which then can only be followed by social fragmentation, thus resulting in the failure of natural social integration by the people who are subjected to this kind of experiment.

I would venture to say that in America the original true definition of the word "nation" is lost and even foreign to many Americans today. Most would say they believe a nation is made up of people, whoever they happen to be, all sharing the same chunk of real estate. But like many things lost and forgotten in this country, so is the true meaning of what a nation really is.

In the *New American Webster College Handy Dictionary* (3rd edition), we find two definitions of the word – nation. The original and natural definition of the word "nation" is listed first.

1. Nation: A race of people having common decent, language, and culture.

This "nation" described in definition #1 is what is commonly called the "organic nation" that has a defined natural historic common culture. This is what all historic nations basically used to be and that is the way God willed man to create them in the first place with His actions in Genesis 11. Why do I call definition #1 the natural definition of the word nation? Just take another look at this definition and then ask yourself whats unnatural about it? Now lets look at definition #2, the next added definition of the word "nation" in this same dictionary.

2. Nation: A body of people constituting a political unit or under one government.

So let's ask the question: Where did definition #2 of the word "nation" come from? Did it historically come from the Germans in

Germany? Did it come from the historic French from France? Did the Chinese think it up? No, they didn't. The fact is definition #2 must follow the original definition #1 in this dictionary. Why? Because a natural nation is created by the natural cultural process and it can only be followed by the type of nation which is "unnaturally" created." To use an example: Can you imagine say 2000 years ago some Germans, some Chinese, and the African Hutu tribe, all coming together on their own free will to create a body of people so they can form a political unit and be under one government? This type of unnatural nation in definition #2 can only be created by governments and institutions and not by the free will of man or by God Himself. Today the description of the unnatural nation in definition #2 can be attached to many nations in Europe, including America herself. This second type of nation is affectionately called by the elites – The Multicultural Nation. And what a multicultural nation is not is definition #1 – A race of people having common descent, language, and culture.

~ The Natural Attachment to Soil ~

Terms such as, the old neighborhood, hometown, and down home, are terms of affection given to a chunk of real estate which is familiar to an individual. It's a point of reference regarding a place that is local or fondly remembered as used to being local. Man being a creature of habit likes to have familiarity with his surroundings. He likes to have a place he can call his home. A place he knows he is emotionally, physically, and yet even historically a part of. To be attached to ones surroundings is a natural part of being human. Soil will always be an important element in all peoples existence. Your attachment to soil rests on five levels of existence.

It all begins with our sense of home. The place where your fondest memories are made and the most important decisions in your life will be decided. Family birthdays, holidays, and raising your children all happen within the walls of your home. It includes the yard you mow and that garden you were supposed to plant last spring.

The next level of attachment is the neighborhood. A place where the children play games, friends are made, and where summer evening walks are taken with your pet of choice. Its the place that had that window across the way that you had to fix after your slugger knocked his ball over the fence.

Your next sense of attachment is your town or city. The place where you usually work and play. This includes schools, churches, and local government. It was at this level that the government voting began, which for some strange reason seemed to coincide with those headaches you started getting.

Your next stop on attachment is your state. Yes, it was you who said that your college football team could whip your brothers college football team back in 2013. It is in the state where many work trades must be approved and certified. It includes those vacations, weekend getaways, and the bear at the State park that will never forget you.

Finally, your last sense of attachment rests on your nation. That place at the Federal level with that all unifying flag. The place that you will name when you tell that Brazilian where you are from when traveling.

All these five places listed have one common denominator running under them and that is soil. A soil that you as a citizen of a nation are familiar with and have a sense of belonging to. A piece of dirt you have walked on most of your life. A type of soil that means something different to you at each interconnected level. Once that soil has been claimed by a nation of people, they will develop it, it will sustain their lives, and in the end they will defend it to the death.

~ **Kinism, the natural attachment to ones own** ~

Kinism defined means: *The belief that the ordained social order for man is tribal and ethnic rather than imperial and universal, and focuses on a duty to love ones own people. That Mankind was designed by God to live in extended family groups.*

What this definition is saying is that it is natural for a person to be attached to ones own blood and race as God ordained it to be. It exemplifies definition #1 of the word "nation." That statement will be high fived by many Blacks, Mexicans, Jews, Muslims, and other American minorities, but it will cause many persons of Whiteness to withdraw in fear or cross their eyes in confusion. Today the mere mention of blood and race brings visions of pointy white hats and swastikas to the Caucasian, "but" only when their race is considered mind you. Mention race to the Caucasian when referring to minorities and you'll see the quick smile, a reassuring nod, and his right hand swiftly making its way to his back pants pocket to retrieve his wallet for a donation. But isn't it true though in America we not only encourage Kinism but we actually promote it and celebrate it as evidenced by the many annual multicultural events recognized in this country? So is the Kinist to be put in the same boat as a racist?

Merriam-Webster dictionary: Racist: Poor treatment of or violence against people because of their race.

Looking back at the definition of Kinism you will not find the words – poor treatment, violence, or even prejudice or discrimination. The descriptive words used for Kinism is – love, duty, family. So the question is, is Kinism alive and well in multicultural America?

The Black Kinist: Can a Black man be viewed as a practicing racist if he prefers the company of his own racial type to the company of others? One would have to look long and hard to find someone who thinks like that. As a race the Blacks understand the politics of cultural division and even though they may have come from different regions or even different tribes from their original homeland this crew usually operates as one on America's soil. If a guy named Al Sharpton says some brothers were wrongly accused of violence in Jena, Louisiana, in 2006, by God 20,000 Blacks will make the trip to defend their blood. While I cannot agree with the reasoning for their protest in Jenna, I remain impressed with these people who stand shoulder to shoulder in support of each other in most situations. Blacks can usually be counted on to vote in a Democratic block, and if polled you'll find them generally on the same side of most issues. These people have their own slang terms, their own music, and even some unique dishes that they can claim as their own. Today Blacks promote themselves as a race above their citizenship here in America with the term they not only label themselves with but have caused all others to use when formally addressing them as a people. That label is: African American. This leaves you with the impression that their African race title is placed first, above, and in front of their American citizenship. Now granted it helps Blacks to have an adoring press in their corner who work tirelessly to promote their race and with a massive infusion of government programs over the decades this crew has made impressive economic advancements in this country. The African American can be counted on as a strong Kinist within this multicultural country.

The Mexican Kinist: You can count on the Mexican people to be equally as strong as the Black race with regards to blood. It took a while but now the media and the government has decided it's their turn and these people are making impressive strides in all areas of American life. This crowd usually skips the label of Mexican American and are mostly referred to as just Mexicans. This bunch is so numerically dominant in America that they seem to swallow up all other Latin American immigrants from the South American continent causing them all usually to be referred to as Mexicans. Today the Mexican illegal alien can march on this nations soil and demand the host people to hand over their country to them as a present and absolutely get away with it right on national television. This crew makes little secret about their plans to reclaim America's Southwest from the gringo. Just ask any Mexican from Texas to California where his loyalties lie and many times you will get an answer from south of the border. Now granted, like the Blacks, it sure helps to have an adoring press and U.S. Government support, but also having La Raza, their premier organization being funded by the Ford Foundation and Bill Gates, as it tries to figure out how to Reconquista the Southwest doesn't hurt either.

But beyond the media and monetary support the Mexicans can be credited with not only maintaining their language and their unique customs in a foreign country but actually causing the host nation to adopt Spanish as a second language. The Mexican people are a fine example of what a Kinist is.

The Jewish Kinist: The Jews in America are only around 3% of the general population but look out! You'll find these people among the wealthy of the country and racially over represented in the legal, and entertainment industries. They have their own religion, their own language, and their own unique culture fully intact and hitting on all cylinders within the borders of this multicultural nation. From influencing political parties to running Hollywood, these people can move mountains when their interest arises. They vote mostly in a democratic block and if polled you'll generally find them on the liberal side of the fence. These Jewish Americans are probably one of the best examples of what a Kinist is today.

The Asian Kinist: Now how about that Asian population? Now to be fair there are many different types of Asians here and they prefer to be viewed racially separate from others of the same persuasion. The Mexicans may have mostly swallowed up America's Latino population but not so with the Asian crowd. There are Japanese, Chinese, Koreans, Vietnamese, Malaysians, Hawaiians, to name some of the bigger Asian populations here in America. They may look similar to us but don't call a Filipino a Japanese or vice versa. Now these Asians for the most part are thought of as hard working clannish businessmen. Since they are viewed by most here as an economic success they are almost never referred to as a minority in the same sense that Blacks and Mexicans are. You'll find the Asian many times carving out a chunk of town for themselves and eventually by racial default those places will acquire names such as Chinatown, Korea town, etc. They are just practicing that form of Kinism as human beings as they are acting on that natural instinct by seeking out the comfort of their own to live with. Even a globalist should understand this instinct as long as he doesn't apply it to the Caucasian.

The Arab Kinist: Let's look at that American Arab population. These people rode into town from many different Arab states harnessed to an Islamic religion that is so dominant that it has become the main glue that unites most Arabs as a unique people. They build houses of worship called Mosques just about everywhere they migrate to and much of their social life is centered around these places. But many times this same religion is a reason for conflict within multicultural America and other European nations. The one thing you will never see is a Muslim trying to water down his religion for the appeasement of the host country he has landed in. Where you will find this crew is on the front lines defending Islam and their original home turf through organizations such as CAIR or by other means less attractive to the lovers of peace. But on balance you'll find the Arab practicing his own form of Kinism wherever he migrates to.

The Indian Kinist: We are all familiar with much of the American Indian culture as it has been played out for decades in the Cinema as one of this country's favorite movie themes. The Indians, like the Blacks, now promote themselves as a race above their host country with the more recently self-proclaimed label of – Native American. Since they are recognized as a separate nation within the borders of America this title actually fits. This resilient people are tough and cling to many of the old ways of their tribes original cultural past. They still maintain many of their languages as they live separately on reservations. Kinists? No doubt. It's blood first with this crew and they could care less if you don't like it.

But then there are those others. You know, those White ones that claimed to have settled this Nation and laid the original cultural ground work for what this country was founded on. Can these people be Kinists? Yes, as much as anyone I reckon. But these White ones, like the minorities are also separated into subgroups such as Germans, Italians, French, Irish, English, and others. The original founding American citizens from the United Kingdom can even be subdivided into four basic groups with the English, Irish, Scottish, and Welsh. Is it natural for the Caucasian to be drawn to his own people also? Of course, but unlike the minorities in America, the people of the paler complexion tend to run into racial trouble when they practice some of that tribal exclusion of Kinism here.

Using the political example of the Tea Party movement. It has been described as an all White racist group by some in the liberal media because this political party has a majority of Whites in their ranks. The Tea Party is not a European race cultural movement but a political party organized to fight reckless government spending and the Obama Healthcare takeover and is open to all who wish to join. Nevertheless and typical, if the live bodies in the organization are White, it is many times labeled as racist by the media.

The White majority population when including all European ethnicities in America generally find it more difficult to be viewed as Kinists when they are together than other races because while the government and the media both work in concert to elevate the minority cultures, they at the same time discourage any type of positive recognition of the historically once dominant European Christian culture in America. Isn't it true today that the Black man can look across a table at a fellow Black stranger and recognize an established a racial bond? You can probably make the claim that most minorities in this country have an unspoken racial bond. But as Americans of European races may be proud as individuals of their old country's heritage, they tend not to recognize a blood connection with an individual from a different European country.

My point is that many minorities of this nation have bridged the historical cultural division of their ancient tribal ethnicities and have molded into one American racial group in many ways while the White today is actually racially discouraged from doing the same thing within his own nation. This splinters the political will of the European American causing him to act socially and politically as an individual in many ways while the minority can act socially and politically as a group.

~ The unconnected global citizen ~

The next logical step for the multicultural citizen to take is into global citizenship. Ever heard that term batted around before? Today you will hear some local High School Superintendents at PTA meetings informing the parents how his school is preparing your child for global citizenship. Does that comment inspire warm fuzzies? Will you start to think back on how nice it has been since you became a citizen of the world these last few years? Does being part of the global culture inspire fond memories? Were you thinking global when you reminisced about the time you taught your son how to ride a bide down that old dirt road in Kentucky? Were you a good global citizen when you participated in that bake sale to help raise funds for the new gym at the local High School? I will bet you cannot recall one time you can look back with fond memories of globalism. But I'll make that same wager you have many fond memories of driving in the country thinking how beautiful your state is. You see, man must be connected to his culture by not only blood but also by soil. You did not help your daughter sell Girl Scout cookies in Bangladesh last year, that sale happened in a place called home.

The pride and joy of globalism called the European Union or the EU can never be a true nation. It has no language, no familiar songs about it, and no cultural Plays about its history. All it is and can ever be is a political economic agreement between signatory European nations. It is the Webster definition #2 of what a nation is. The power this Union has over the European nations is socially dysfunctional at best since there is no social function and economically not much better. The European debt crisis, often referred to as the Eurozone crisis or the European sovereign debt crisis is a multi-year debt crisis that has been taking place in the European Union since the end of 2009. Several Eurozone member states, Greece, Portugal, Ireland, Spain, and Cyprus, were unable to repay or refinance their government debt or to bail out over-indebted banks under their national supervision without the assistance of third parties like other EU countries, the European Central Bank (ECB) or the International Monetary Fund (IMF). This economic inter-connectedness means that when Spain gets the flu, the rest of the participating EU countries get a cold. As I write these words Britain has just voted to leave the EU. This stunning turn of events was accompanied by a plunge in the financial markets worldwide. And now another five European countries now want a referendum to vote on their future membership in the EU. Nobel Prize winner for economics *Milton Friedman* said regarding the EU's monetary system, "the euro is going to be a big source of problems, not a source of help. To the best of my knowledge there has never been a monetary union putting out a fiat currency composed of independent states. There have been unions based on gold and silver, but not on fiat money."

Pat Buchanan in his book, *State of Emergency*, says, "for a nation to endure, its people must form a moral and social community and share higher values than just legal and economic interests." He's right. Can you envision an Italian getting all misty eyed when describing his love for the European Union? Who can forget the French people in WWII shouting, Vive la France! How long do you think you will be waiting before you hear some Dane say "long live the European Union!" There just is no emotional attachment to a governmental entity that is based solely on laws and money. Why? Because you cannot touch it, feel it, smell it, or walk on it. A girl may be delighted to say "my fiance took me to Paris and asked me to marry him." But you will not hear her say, my fiance took me to the European Union to ask that same question.

It's always been about blood and soil and the farther the elites steer us away from that natural way of thinking the more we understand it by the ramifications of its absence. For multiculturalism to take root it must absolutely eliminate the concept of the individuals natural attachment to ones own people and ones own turf. To put it another way, the defined goal of the elites is that they must spiritually and emotionally detach the national citizen from the very roots of himself and his natural environment to effect the global change desired. If successful, the result of this unnatural detachment will be the birth of a rootless detached soul who will be left searching for something to spiritually and emotionally re-attach himself to. It is within this manufactured void where the elites promote their spiritual replacement called globalism. But man being a creature of habit with a need for natural attachments to things he is familiar with will always rebel against the unfamiliar. This is the spiritual and emotional dichotomy that multiculturalism produces.

A DIVIDED (MULTICULTURAL) NATION SHALL NOT STAND

The division in America today is vast and growing. For any thinking person to question that truth can only exhibit their ignorance to the highest degree. Today this country is divided on critical issues such as race, religion, language, history, laws, social norms, sexual identity, and just about every other cultural issue you can dig up. There are civil rights for the benefit of some and affirmative action programs that exclude others. From ESL programs (English as a second language) that promote foreign languages over English, to hate crime laws that add extra penalties if the crime is thought to be racially motivated. Don't forget those speech codes in Universities to keep certain words from being uttered on campus that may offend students of certain races, genders, or sexual orientations. But then isn't that what our global masters in the government want? Isn't that what multiculturalism delivers when it is forced upon the original host majority? A divided culture of instability? But isn't a divided country weaker and more easily controlled?

~ **Has there ever been such a divided country?** ~

What causes cultural and racial division in a country? When different cultures and races are represented en masse within the same geographical borders you of course will get division. Now let me remind you that historically the nations of the world were much more racially homogeneous than they are today. Yes, much to the chagrin of the elites of the world, people with the same genetic codes historically and even naturally drifted together and formed their own cultures and nations for the amazingly simple reason it was easier and more convenient to come together with someone who was like themselves. That is the way things normally progressed for a millennia until one day that elite bunch with too much money and time on their hands got itchy, restless, and generally unsatisfied with being the leaders of the richest and most successful nations in the world and began promoting their social experiment called multiculturalism.

Now I won't go too deep into the Roman version of multiculturalism. We are all basically aware that Rome ended up being the most powerful empire of its time for hundreds of years only to end their reign by a self-inflicted multicultural disaster. But hey, why should history be our judge and jury today? Now is it a trusim that people of the same race but of a different ethnicity will famously get along within a common border? Not really and not always if there is an ethnic division. Look no further than at Northern Ireland at the ongoing conflict between the Irish Catholics and the Scottish Protestants. The origins of the ethnic and cultural differences between the Irish and the Scottish lie in the fact that the two groups never could integrate properly in the first place. In terms of ethnicity, the Irish Catholics in general see themselves as descendants of the Gaelic people native to Ireland while the Scots were settlers relocated by King James I of England in the 16th Century during the historic plantations period to actually provide a territorial buffer zone of sorts for the British. This plantation strategy was intended to prevent further Irish rebellion as over the preceding century Ireland had proven to be the region most resistant to English control. So there you have two racially White peoples when combined together within a common border were divided over ethnicity, geography, and religion, to the point of open warfare. These three cultural elements have been enough to keep these two groups producing casualties for over one hundred years.

What about the genocidal disaster in Rwanda Africa between the Hutu and Tutsi tribes in 1994? On balance these tribes were of the same race with the Tutsi tribesmen being notably a physically taller tribe. It was the Tutsi who historically migrated into the smaller Hutu tribesmen lands and eventually integrated with them. Here the cultural differences were ethnic, physical, and historically geographical, but it was still enough to cause a death toll in the Rwanda massacre that shocked the world.

But this is the same problem encountered in various degrees between different ethnic peoples throughout history. They may be of the same race, even speak the same language, live together for a duration, and have even intermarried, yet they still hated each other in just enough ways beneath the emotional surface to eventually produce a level of conflict. Both these historic examples just given show that time will not always erase ones ethnicity, ones culture, ones history, and especially ones pride in who their fathers were and who they claim to be today.

~ The melting pot vs. the salad bowl ~

There was a time in America when we had what was once called a "melting pot." This meant that all these incoming "European immigrants" from all over the world were encouraged and even expected to assimilate into the host British American culture. It seemed to work fine for a couple hundred years for these following reasons. Most of these immigrants were of the same Caucasian race, basically had the same religion, a common set of values, and even common holidays. So with that much culturally in common already these European immigrants were eager and easy to assimilate. Hence the term: The "melting pot" was born.

Then somewhere in the 1960's along came a spider. The multicultural spider that is. This spider crept in slowly and quietly and death was on his mind. The death of America as all who knew her.

> ....*Now this spider looked around one day and saw all these happy pasty white faces and realized he couldn't do what he wanted to do which was control the world unless he divided it first so he then said, "you Americans have worked and built this great nation of yours into an economic powerhouse and it's just not fair to the other races of the world.*

What's not fair? said Mr. White.

Its not fair that you have so much and others have so little. So I, says the multicultural spider, am going to have to change a few things around here. For starters lets get rid of that outdated melting pot and replace it with something more progressive. Something I call a salad bowl.

What's a salad bowl? asked Mr. White.

> *Well said the spider, it means the pot, which is now a bowl, will no longer have anything melting in it. It will have a bunch of different things in it, kind of like a salad does, but a salad doesn't melt in a salad bowl, its just all in there together but at the same time all different, get it?*

Will we like the salad? asked Mr. White.

> *Funny, said the multicultural spider, I don't remember asking.*

And so here we are today. No longer the European melting pot but a conglomeration of competing races, cultures, ethnicities, languages, histories, religions, with different values, traditions, customs, and even different and conflicting holidays. This means one cherished holiday in one culture can be a vial curse to another. One set of customs in one culture just might be an abomination to another. One honored part of history to one culture just might be cause for damnation by another.

> *Ah says the multicultural spider as he looks down on his creation today. I think the new slogan for my America will be – diversity is our strength.*

* ~ And God said: The people is one ~ *

And now Gods ancient judgment revealed

At this time I will reveal where I found my authority for this book. An ancient biblical judgment so cataclysmic the world's course was altered forever. A judgment all theologians are aware of but due to the historic transition of the original bible teachings into the modern multicultural love theology of today, they have over time lost sight of this judgments true significance, therefore rendering these modern day theologians unable to apply its original message to the present Christian era.

What does God have to say about multiculturalism? Does He promote it? Does He bless it or does He condemn it? Genesis 11, tells us that God does not approve of the races coming together at all. It is in this bible book where the most profound statement on this subject can be found.

Genesis 11

1, *And the whole earth was of one language, and of one speech.*

4, *And they said, Go to, let us build us a city, and a tower, whose top may reach unto heaven; and let us make us a name, lest we be scattered abroad upon the face of the whole earth.*

5, *And the LORD came down to see the city and the tower, which the children of men builded.*

6, *And the LORD said, Behold, the people is one, and they have all one language; and this they begin to do: and now nothing will be restrained from them, which they have imagined to do.*

7, *Go to, let us go down, and there confound their language, that they may not understand one another's speech.*

8, *So the LORD scattered them abroad from thence upon the face of all the earth: and they left off to build the city.*

9, *Therefore is the name of it called Babel; because the LORD did there confound the language of all the earth: and from thence did the LORD scatter them abroad upon the face of all the earth*

Do you understand that God was dealing with the first biblical multicultural country here in Genesis 11? Lets break this story down into its basic components.

God identifies the problem:
4, *And they said, Go to, let us build us a city, and a tower, whose top may reach unto heaven;*

God identifies why the people are able to create this problem: (something never taught in church)
6, *And the LORD said, Behold, the people is one, and they have all one language;*

God tells us why it is a problem:
6, *….now nothing will be restrained from them, which they have imagined to do.*

What does God do to solve the problem?
9, *LORD did there confound the language of all the earth: and from thence did the LORD scatter them abroad upon the face of all the earth.*

Gods logical conclusion to the problem man had created was to separate the races so they wouldn't be living near each other and then confounding their languages so they couldn't communicate with each other.

SIDE NOTE: This does not mean one cannot visit a foreign country today or the gospel cannot be taken to other countries by missionaries. The judgment is on races integrating within common borders or simply coming together as one.

Since God considered it logical to separate the races when they were before together, a few questions come to mind.

1. Can it be said that God was displeased by what man could do when all the races of the world came together as one during the time of Genesis?
2. Did God put some sort of time limit on how long His forced separation judgment of the worlds races was to be in effect?
3. Is it "illogical" for man to undo what God considered logical to do in Genesis 11, and once again come together as one in a multicultural nation today?

Those who read the bible know that God did not put a time limit on His judgment of separation of the races of the world during the building of the Tower of Babel. God knows the inner workings of man and in fact He can read our hearts to know us better than we know ourselves. Are we still born sinners in the eyes of God today or were just the people back in Genesis born sinners? In the time of the story of Babel everyone lived together and spoke the same language. This enabled the peoples of the world to be able to pool their intellectual and physical resources since everyone could communicate with everyone else. As a result nothing was impossible for them or could be restrained from them. So can it not be said that to form a multicultural nation today can be viewed as defying the very will of God with regards to His judgment in Genesis 11?

God did not separate the people and change their language because He wanted some elitist to undo His work at a later date did He? God is the creator and He doesn't change His ways to appease some religiously challenged elitist or to pamper some modern preacher man of love theology today. There are some theories out there that the Tower of Babel was actually an attempt to build the first New World Order. Another theory is that this tower was actually built in a specific location to gain access to a known portal into another spiritual dimension leading to Heaven as Genesis 11:4, tell us, *"whose top may reach into the heaven."* Why would the people want to build a tower that could get them to a portal into heaven? The book of *Jasher* which is mentioned in the bible three times goes into deeper detail concerning this Tower of Babel story.

Book of Jasher:

Ch. 9:25, *And the building of the tower was unto them a transgression and a sin, and they began to build it, and whilst they were building against the Lord God of heaven, they imagined in their hearts **to war against Him and to ascend into heaven**.* (through a portal)

9:26, *And all these people and all the families divided themselves in three parts; the first said We will ascend into heaven and fight against Him; the second said, We will ascend to heaven and place our own gods there and serve them; and the third part said, We will ascend to heaven and smite Him with bows and spears; and God knew all their works and all their evil thoughts, and he saw the city and the tower which they were building.*

9:29, *And the Lord knew their their thoughts, and it came to pass when they were building they cast the arrows toward the heavens, and all the arrows fell upon them filled with blood, and when they saw them they said to each other, Surely we have slain all those that are in heaven.*

So according to the book of *Jasher*, the building of the Tower of Babel was acheived to gain access to heaven to make war on God and to over throw heaven. Gods judgment on the Tower of Babel in the book of *Jasher* was similar to how the book of Genesis tells it.

~ Some claim the Judgment of Babel is no longer in effect ~

Some say that Gods judgment with regards to the tower of Babel is no longer in effect for the reason of the Pentecost. We know the Pentecost as the great festival that marks the birth of the Christian church. The word "church" does not exist in the Old Testament. Before the Pentecost the teachings of the Prophets and Jesus were reserved for the ancient tribes of Israel only. This is evidenced by Jesus Himself in the following scriptures.

Matthew 10: Jesus instructs His apostles who they must minister to:

5, *These twelve Jesus sent forth, and commanded them, saying, Go not into the way of the Gentiles, and into any city of the Samaritans enter ye not:*
6, *but go rather to the lost sheep of the house of Israel.*

Matthew 15:24, *But he answered and said, I am not sent but unto the lost sheep of the house of Israel.*

In Matthew 7, Jesus tells us some were not allowed to have the holy teachings.

6, *Give not that which is holy unto the dogs, neither cast ye your pearls before swine, lest they trample them under their feet, and turn again and rend you.*

So for the sake of brevity we are just going to have to take Christs word for it that the gospel was only for the lost tribes of Israel during

His time and before. In Matthew 16:18 the word "church" finally makes its appearance twice but still hasn't been created yet.

Matt. 16:18,

> *And I say also unto thee, That thou art Peter, and upon this rock I will build my church; and the gates of hell shall not prevail against it.*

The church is not mentioned again until the book of Acts 2. It is here that the celebration of the Pentecost took place and the word "church" appears over 10 times. The creation of the church meant for the first time that the Gentiles were now able to receive the Holy Ghost through Christ and the gospel through the Apostles.

Acts 2:

1, *And when the day of Pentecost was fully come, they were all with one accord in one place.*

4, *And they were all filled with the Holy Ghost, and began to speak with other tongues, as the Spirit gave them utterance.*

6, *Now when this was noised abroad, the multitude came together, and were confounded, because that every man heard them speak in his own language.*

8, *And how hear we every man in our own tongue, wherein we were born?*

9, *Par'thi-ans, and Medes, and E'lamites, and the dwellers in Mesopota'mi-a, and in Judea, and Cappado'cia, in Pontus, and Asia,*

10, *Phryg'i-a, and Pamphyl'i-a, in Egypt, and in the parts of Libya about Cyre'ne, and strangers of Rome, Jews and proselytes,*

11, *Cretes and Arabians, we do hear them speak in our tongues the wonderful works of God.*

38, *Then Peter said unto them, Repent, and be baptized every one of you in the name of Jesus Christ for the remission of sins, and ye shall receive the gift of the Holy Ghost.*

THE LIVING SIN • 139

41, *Then they that gladly received his word were baptized: and the same day there were added unto them about three thousand souls.*

Now this Pentecost phenomenon did not affect everyone because verse 13 in that same chapter tells us: *Others mocking said, these men are full of new wine.* So it is scripturally safe to say about 3000 gentiles received the Holy Ghost and were baptized on the day of Pentecost during the birth of the Christian church. No mention of God rescinding any judgment of separation or reversing His stance on going back to one language on earth, or even telling the world they can now dwell in multicultural nations. In Acts 10, Peter backs up the message that the gentiles can now receive the Holy Ghost but unfortunately this bible story has been viewed incorrectly by many as the end of Gods dietary laws.

Acts 10:

10, *and he became very hungry, and would have eaten: but while they made ready, he fell into a trance,*

11, *and saw heaven opened, and a certain vessel descending unto him, as it had been a great sheet knit at the four corners, and let down to the earth:*

12, *wherein were all manner of fourfooted beasts of the earth, and wild beasts, and creeping things, and fowls of the air.*

13, *And there came a voice to him, Rise, Peter; kill, and eat.*

14, *But Peter said, Not so, Lord; for I have never eaten any thing that is common or unclean.*

15, *And the voice spake unto him again the second time, What God hath cleansed, that call not thou common.*

Right about now is when most Christians think they are smarter than Peter and quickly close the case. They claim to understand that this means one can now eat any animal that was once called unclean because as they view it, the Lord just said He now cleaned them. But if Peter who is talking directly to God doesn't understand what's going on, how can a Christian say they can over 1000 years later?

Acts 10, (con't)

17, *Now while Peter doubted in himself what this vision which he had seen should mean,*

So what is the message God is trying to give us? Peter does eventually figure this out and lets us in on it in this same chapter.

27, *And as he talked with him, he went in, and found many that were come together.*
28, *And he said unto them, Ye know how that it is an unlawful thing for a man that is a Jew* (ancient Israel) *to keep company, or come unto one of another nation;* **but God hath showed me that I should not call any man common or unclean.**

The message is clear. Peter finally figured out that the animals in the vision represented "formerly unclean people/gentiles" which now have been cleansed by God. To understand this message just review the words "common and unclean" and how they are used three times in this chapter. What this all means is that the Gentiles (non-tribes of Israel) now were able to be baptized and receive the Holy Ghost.

44, *While Peter yet spake these words, the Holy Ghost fell on all them which heard the word.*
45, *And they of the circumcision which believed were astonished, as many as came with Peter, because that on the Gentiles also was poured out the gift of the Holy Ghost.*

So again can you find anywhere in this chapter God rescinding His judgment of racial separation here in Acts 10? Receiving the Holy Ghost and being baptized has nothing to do with the tribes of world once again coming together as one. Seems the Gentiles to this day are still speaking different languages which can only mean no one world language was brought back by the arrival of the Pentecost. So it should be clear to all God did not rescind the Genesis 11, language judgment. At the Pentecost did God say in any way that some type of multicultural nation is now okay by Him? Did He order the people of the world to once again move back together as one as they were before His judgment on the Tower of Babel? You can pour over Acts 2 and 10 all day long and you will not find anything remotely resembling any type of Godly judgment rescind. God also did not say He was going to rescind just the physical separation judgment of Babel while still keeping the language barriers in place did He? He didn't say His original judgment of separation was only temporary did He? God had no trouble communicating to the world when He ended the old covenant He gave to Moses when He replaced it with a new covenant. He was very clear in Genesis when He promised He would never flood the world again by setting His bow (rainbow) in the sky as a promise. A person is going to have to be reaching and reaching pretty far if they want to claim that the Tower of Babel judgment is over because of the birth of the church at Pentecost. They would have to insert a lot of words into scripture that does not exist to make that happen in their minds. For me the Pentecost is exactly what the bible says it is. The day the gentiles could be baptized and receive the Holy Ghost. A wonderful thing. A one time event with nothing said about God re-introducing racial integration or a linguistic judgment reversal.

Now that being said, I am fully aware that with minimal effort the bible can be twisted to reflect just about any personal religious view or theology desired by anyone with a bible, a bag of potato chips, and a spare evening. We all know this by the many competing Christian denominations out there today and the multiple versions of the bible. But from my experience of traditional church teachings of the story of the Tower of Babel you'll just about always catch the preacher stopping at the point of mans sin of building this tower. He'll tell you how awful man was for trying to act like God, but right there is where they stop teaching and start preaching. For some reason the priest or preacher is not interested or they are avoiding delving into the reason "why" man was able to build this tower. This is the real story. God does His best to help you out as much as He can by telling you the reason why man was able to build this tower and that is because "The people was one!" That there is the heart of the problem of why God had to act. Look, God already knows we as His creations are sinners. We also know from the bible that if say Bill, as an *individual* in New York City commits a sin, God is not going to go pick Bill up and relocate him to China and cause him to speak Mandarin. The real problem is when people of different races get together. God knows then at that point and has even told us that man gains the ability to have nothing restrained from him and he can begin to do anything he imagines to do. This is the reason God judged man for building the Tower of Babel. This is the reason He separated the races and changed their language. Because of what man was able to do when he came together as one.

This scripture in Genesis 11, on the story of the Tower of Babel is a complete story with a beginning, middle, and end. The chapter leading into the story, Genesis 10, lists the descendants of Noah right up to where the Tower of Babel story starts. The scripture following this story lists the descendants of Shem and Terah. There is nothing confusing about the way this story is presented. It is an uninterrupted story with no fuzzy parables and no prophesies. Its so simple even an elite caveman can understand it.

~ From nation/state citizen to multiculturalist to globalist ~

Can we apply this biblical story in Genesis 11, to America today? The Christian can and should. Why is this story of the Tower of Babel even more relevant to our lives today? Look no further than what kind of mischief man is getting himself into now. Witness how he is coming together from all nations of the world to America. Witness the many world organizations man has created and a European Union to boot. It must be understood that one short step away from the Multiculturalist you'll find the Globalist. And the globalist's reasons for existence is to replace the God created traditional nation/state citizen with a Global oriented person that will worship at the alter of some type of World Government. It's all about power from control. National power controls nations but global power is something else isn't it? Answer this question. If the Globalists get their way everyone will be a global citizen. If everyone becomes a global citizen then can I make the claim that once again....*the people are one*?

The reason why we know there are individuals with a desire for global power is by the creation of a multitude of world organizations that are working in concert to reduce in status the power and sovereignty of the nation/state in order to elevate in status a world governing entity some call: The New World Order.

Now here is where the skeptic starts leaning back in his chair hemming and hawing about me being some type of conspiracy theorist. Well then I guess I am about as much a conspiracy theorist as many of your recent Presidents are. In Leo Hohmann's *Worldnetdaily article* on February 4, 2016, he cites George Bush the senior, George W. Bush the junior, and Bill Clinton, all using the term, New World Order. Other notables such as Jeb Bush and Henry Kissinger were included in this NWO verbalize. In fact it seems a whole lot of important people that have some sort of interest in this form of government also made the list in this article. In this link there are 37 quotes from world notables all expressing their desire for, or knowledge of – a New World Order.

https://endtimesprophecyreport.com/2013/06/05/new-world-order-37-quotes-on-the-new-world-order/

On this list you will also find Richard Nixon, the Rockefellers, Mikhail Gorbachev, Saul Alinsky, Dwight D. Eisenhower, Tony Blair, and even a Robert Kennedy, just to name a few.

Seems our latest President was speaking at a fundraiser in a wealthy enclave of Seattle in 2014, and as reported: *Obama* said, "there is a sense among Americans that around the world the old order isn't holding and we're not quite where we need to be in terms of a new order that's based on a different set of principles."

Well butter my butt and call me a biscuit!

You will know this global crowd by their deeds and actions. You'll find them lurking in world organizations on down to even local governments parroting legislative nasties such as Agenda 21, advocating for open borders, and promoting global economics. There are too many global organizations to list but here is the short list of their most important vehicles of enforced world change.

- The CFR, or the Council on Foreign Relations: Known to some as the invisible fourth branch of the United States Government. You'll find this organization filled with America's top ranked globalists with names such as Henry Kissinger, Alan Greenspan, Paul Volker, and the late Tony Snow, to name a few. This is the crew behind projects such as "Building a North American Community" that includes Canada, and Mexico, while also promoting another organization called, "Security and Prosperity Partnership of North America" which again involves the same three nations.
- The UN, or the United Nations: The title of this organization tells us all we need to know about this global entity.
- The WHO, or the World Health Organization: This is a specialized agency established in 1948 by the United Nations that acts as an international coordinating authority on public health.

This is the dysfunctional keystone cop organization that upgraded the so called H1N1 Swine Flu so called pandemic to the threat to level 6 in 2009.

UPDATE: This same WHO led the charge in the Covid 19 Plandemic of 2020 and milked it for everything they could including masks that don't work, social distancing in the name of fear promoted by their mainstream press, to the Covid 19 shot which is an MRA technology which has killed and maimed millions worldwide. This shot that was never properly tested for safety and never approved by the FDA was pushed out as an EUA (emergency use authorization) which removed any liability for doctors and pharmacists and the companies that created these shots. Unashamed and pressing onward the World Health Assembly which is the governing body of The World Health Organization will meet in Switzerland to discuss the next steps for its pandemic treaty [and its] quest to use public health to expand The WHO's power over sovereign states.

- The WTO, or the World Trade Organization: This is an international organization designed by its founders to supervise and liberalize international trade. Many have pointed out that this entity is trying to do an end run around the American constitution by way of international treaties.
- The World Bank: This banks mission statement is to reduce poverty and improve the living standards among various nations by promoting sustainable growth and investment in people. Because direct colonial control of the world is no longer tolerated, the elites need an indirect way to control policies implemented by foreign governments. By getting these foreign governments onto the debt treadmill and promising them new cash if they implement their policies, this World Bank gains economic control of target countries.

- The IMF, or the International Monetary Fund: This entity works to ensure there is order in international monetary relations. It also oversees the international monetary system to ensure exchange rate stability and to encourage member countries to eliminate exchange restrictions that hinder trade. When a signatory state in the European Union economically bogs down it is the feared IMF that will gladly pay them a visit.
- NAFTA, or the North American Free Trade Agreement: This organization was created in 1993 to expand trade between the U.S., Canada, and Mexico, and to make them more competitive in the global market place. Its main goal was to reduce trade barriers with Canada and more importantly with Mexico. By 2005 it was estimated that NAFTA was responsible for eliminating over one million U.S. jobs as reported by the Economic Policy Institute. Yes it was you who were wisely warned about NAFTA in 1992 by Yoda's doppelganger – Ross Perot, of "that great sucking sound you will hear will be the sound of American jobs being sucked out of our country by Mexico."
- CAFTA, or the Central American Free Trade Agreement: Building on the stunning success of President Clintons NAFTA, President Bush the junior, twisted some Congressional arms to create CAFTA in 2005 to extend NAFTA's ugly step sister all the way down to Chile to give the American worker some more of that SHAFTA!

Things like building a New World Order could never happen if the worlds people remained in their separate nations as God intended them to be by reason of His actions in Genesis 11. God has already shown us how displeased He was with man the last time they all got together and started a building project. Why He even had the story written down so we could use it as a reference so we would know what ticks Him off. But we as Americans know better don't we? Why we live in modern times now. That old bible story just doesn't apply to us.

Still not convinced of how naugthty man can be when he gets together with his world buddies? Lets see what else these globalists have taken off the back burner and moved to the front. Witness that world creation of what is called "The Hadron Collider." On November 19, 2009, *Earthfiles* internet magazine, gives us the story of CERN. This stands for Council for European Nuclear Research. "Beginning Friday night on the border between Switzerland and France not far from Geneva and three hundred feet underground is the Hadron Collider. Humans will try again to start producing subatomic energies close to those believed to be in the Big Bang Theory." Earthfiles reports that the CERN organization is made up of sixty European member states. What might come out of the high energy collisions being produced by the Collider could be the elusive "Higgs Boson Particle" that has never been detected but which physicists "think" is responsible for the mass of every particle and is the key to cosmic construction." Thats why the Higgs Boson Particle is affectionately known as the God Particle. Says theoretical physicist Michio Kaku, "this machine will help us unlock the secret of the origin of the universe." Well well well, add this to the Big Bang Theory and you have two unprovable scientific theories occupying these glassy eyed Einstein minds. Actually the Big Bang Theory is a creationist theory that was thought up in 1933 by a Catholic Priest by the name of George Lemaitre and believe it or not this theory is still promoted today by cosmologists.

In the bible it says in Genesis 1:1 – 2, *In the beginning God created the heaven and earth,* This scripture doesn't say anything about Bangs or Bosons at all does it? I believe there are two possible reasons for the creation of the Hadron Collider. First is that if this crew "in their minds" can prove this Big Bang Theory and tell us they found this Higgs Boson Particle by way of the Hadron Collider, they think they will be able to show the world that man can create his own universe "which in their minds" will prove that either man has no use for God, or that God did not create the universe as told in the book of Genesis.

Outside of the CERN building is a statue of the Hindu god, Lord Shiva the destroyer, who represents the divine force of destruction. Some wonder why they chose this deity for the symbol of CERN. Many conspiracy theorists are very concerned about the CERN project and this is the second possible reason for the creation of the Hadron Collider. Author Michael Tsarion puts forward the theory that "the beings described in the bible as the Nephilim were aliens and that they had been pursued here from another part of the universe and imprisoned within a star gate to put the Earth in quarantine." Michael believes that these beings lost their advanced technologies when Atlantis was destroyed and that ever since they have been working using humans to rebuild the machines and technology they need. Their plan according to Tsarion is to eventually blast through the star gate that holds them prisoner here." Could this be the real reason for the large Hadron Collider? Following are two pictures of Lord Shiva the Destroyer. Actually looks like he is in a star gate or portal of some kind. The first picture is the actual statue of Shiva at CERN.

THE LIVING SIN • 149

Shiva

On September 3, 2015, a Michigan newspaper, *The Daily Reporter,* ran an article claiming that the Hadron Collider was being used as a star gate.

The *UK Express,* had this to say about the Collider on October 22, 2015, "Scientists conducting a mind bending experiment at the Large Hadron Collider next week hope to connect with a Parallel Universe outside of our own."

ZenGardner.com, reports on December 4, 2015, CERN, Stargate of the Shiva? Compares the Collider to the Ancient Egyptian device called the – Ta-Wer, which was a mystic symbol that represented the connection between Abydos and some mythical place in the underworld, interpreted as the "Land of the Dead."

Bibliotecapleyades,net, had this to say about CERN. "Like the pyramids, the CERN LHC which some compare to the Tower of Babel is a Gateway to God.

This mystery has even bubbled up to the elite *Wall Street Journal*, which has had to circle the wagons in hopes of doing major damage control on the conspiracies surrounding this thing. As reported on April 4, 2016, "CERN is seeking secrets of the universe, or maybe opening the portal of Hell."

> *Saphirethronemysteries, had this to say, "The CERN constructed on the Swiss border with France was built on top of an ancient temple to the god Apollo. Romans believed this temple of Apollo was set over the bottomless pit. The bottomless pit is also called the abyss or the underworld. Revelation 9:11 tells us that Abaddon/Apollo is the angel who rules as king over the bottomless pit. Abaddon (Hebrew), is Apollo/Apollyon (Greek), and Shiva (Hindu) are all gods of destruction. Sitting outside the main quarters at CERN is a statute of the Hindu god Shiva. This "god" is said to destroy everything at the molecular level; and then, puts it back together again to give birth to a New World Order – a new golden age."*

All these listed articles and many more are making the claim that this Hadron Collider is not what they are telling us it is. Is man yet again coming together as one and is history repeating itself? Let's connect the dots of what these listed CERN articles are telling us. **Nephilim, Star Gate, Parallel Universe, Tower of Babel, Gateway to God, Apollo, bottomless pit, New World Order**. Theories? Yes, but something seems to be cooking three hundred feet below the earth near Geneva and having the strange Hindu god Shiva the Destroyer, for CERNs symbol adds no comfort to these theories.

Oh and lets not forget what *2paragraphs* said on September 24, 2015, "CERN emphasizes that it is a "Multicultural Institution" with scientists from more than 100 countries, which now includes the U.S. and other non European countries." As was the Tower of Babel a world building project, so is CERN a world building project.

~ Is the Old Testament still relevant? ~

I, for one find myself thinking that since the story of the Tower of Babel is in the Old Testament many Christians are going to fall back on the old argument that it is no longer relevant to modern Christian theology of today. They will make the claim that Christians are now under the new covenant and what happened in Genesis 11, no longer applies to them. These types of Christians tend to look at the Old Testament from a purely historical standpoint only. But does that mean everything God did or what the prophets foretold in the OT is irrelevant? Why is there an Old Testament in the first place then? Why teach anyone the ten commandments which were first introduced in the OT if the book doesn't count? Why teach the creation of the world by God since it also happened in the OT? Do we even need to know the story of Moses? The question for us all is: Are there important lessons to be learned from the OT that are useful to the Christian today?

Is there no lesson to be learned from the story of Noah and the flood? Does not Jesus reference the story of Noah in Matthew 24?

24:37, *But as the days of Noah were, so shall also the coming of the Son of man be.*

So how could we ever understand Christs future prophesy if we didn't study the story of Noah in the OT? Is there no lesson to be learned about what happened to the cities of Sodom and Gomorrah? Does not Jesus refer to Sodom and Gomorrah in Matthew 10, as He addressed His apostles?

Matthew 10:15, *Verily I say unto you, It shall be more tolerable for the land of Sodom and Gomor'rah in the day of judgment, than for that city.*

So how could we ever make some kind of comparison of Christs prophesy if we didn't study this OT story? This time lets leave out the "is there no lesson to be learned" part, and just listen to Peter as he informs the Christian that there is a lesson to be learned from the OT in 2 Peter.

2 Peter 2:6, *and turning the cities of Sodom and Gomor'rah into ashes condemned them with an overthrow, making them an ensample unto those that after should live ungodly;*

So is Peter not telling future Christians that Sodom and Gommorrah should be used as an example and a warning on what not to do? Think Peter is telling us we should know about that OT story? What did Jesus Himself say in Matthew 5?

Matthew 5:17, *Think not that I am come to destroy the law, or the prophets: I am not come to destroy, but to fulfill.*

So according to Jesus we should be studying the law and the prophets words in the OT so we can know what He is going to fulfill right? Just take a look at the worlds current concern of climate change and this so called global warming farce being promoted by the governments of today. Maybe if we looked in the OT in the book of Genesis we could shoot down this phony albatross in one scriptural sentence.

Genesis 8:22, *While the earth remaineth, seedtime and harvest, and cold and heat, and summer and winter, and day and night shall not cease.*

Let the worshipers at the alter of global warming stick that in their legislative train wreck called Cap and Trade. So if Christ Himself tells us we need to understand the Old Testament, who can tell me there can be no lessons learned from the Tower of Babel story? When God separated the races by His judgment wouldn't that mean He wanted them to stay separate? Do practicing Christians today feel they have the authority to invalidate Gods Old Testament judgments and their legitimacy?

~ **Does Jesus warn us about divided nations?** ~

Does Jesus Himself give us any clues that He supports Gods judgment of separation of the nations of the world? Matthew 12, is clear.

Matthew 12:25, *And Jesus knew their thoughts, and said unto them, Every kingdom divided against itself is brought to desolation; and every city or house divided against itself shall not stand:*

Now here again is straight scripture. It is neither a confusing parable nor a prophetic warning and there are no disclaimers or exemptions in His warning. In fact, Jesus keeps using the word "every" to describe who is included in His warning. You won't find one exemption for the modern Christian multicultural nation to crawl under. Jesus did not even put a time limit on this warning. Matthew 12:25, is a straight clear, concise, warning from the Lamb of God for those who have an ear to hear and a mind to obey.

Since a kingdom is a biblical word for what today is a country, can we not say Jesus's warning is for all countries of the world that find themselves divided by whatever the cause may be? Can the claim be made that the multicultural nation by its very existence is a divided nation because of racial differences, its cultural differences, language barriers, religious disparities, historical contrasts, and differing values and customs? Would a thinking Christian come to the conclusion that multicultural America fits the description of what Jesus called – a divided kingdom?

Does Christ give us any clues about how a divided kingdom can fall? In Matthew 24, we find answers.

Matthew 24:7, *For nation shall rise against nation, and kingdom against kingdom: and there shall be famines, and pestilences, and earthquakes, in divers places.*

Let us examine the statement, *"nation shall rise against nation."* A kingdom is a country, but a nation is a race, a distinct people, or a tribe. In this scripture a nation and a kingdom are listed as separate entities. We know a kingdom (country) can attack another kingdom (country) but how could a nation (race) rise against another nation (race) if it wasn't within the same borders with another nation (or race)? If the nation in question was in another kingdom (country) then that description would fall under the statement: *Kingdom against kingdom.* To bring Christs statement in Matthew 24, to its logical conclusion: When a nation rises against another nation, that is what is called in modern times: Race War. Just ponder on Christs words here as our churches continue to sponsor a never ending stream of incoming 3rd world immigrants to the U.S. of A. Have these Pastors found an invisible exemption somewhere in Matthew 12:25?

Is it not true that it is impossible today to say what race an American is? But today is not race dividing this country on many social issues?

Is it not true that we Americans cannot agree as a country on what religion we are? Can any Christian say their religion can be promoted and celebrated in public without either the full force of the law coming down upon him or at least an official condemnation or protest of some sort? Did not President Obama say this country is not a Christian country but a country of many religions? Is it not true that people of different religions in America will ask for the removal of

Christian symbols that are displayed in public? Does that sound like division to you?

Is it not true that America cannot agree on what language it wants to speak? Just call any government office or department store and what two languages will be informing you on which button to push? Go to any small Hispanic or Asian business and you'll probably see their language written on their business sign. It was in 1992 when Congress passed the "voting rights language assistance act" to provide multilingual voting ballots for non-English speakers where ever they may reside in America. Again, sound like a little division going on by way of language?

Is it not true that our European history is being condemned, shut out, canceled, and even attacked by some American Universities on several fronts today? Is not the course Western Civ. either no longer a required subject in many colleges and even considered racist by some?

Is it not true that now our traditional American values and customs are being diluted by multi-racial customs to the point where now the American must be taught to be value neutral, meaning any foreign ethnic custom is just as good and deserving of government protection as the American traditional customs are?

It goes without saying that we cannot even agree on what culture we are just by the very claim that America is multicultural.

Can we say that America promotes division and diversity in the country by encouraging:

- More immigration.
- Promoting public school classes with English as a second language.
- Raising the recognition of foreign religions at the expense of lowering our traditional Christian religion.

- Celebrating multicultural traditions and holidays.
- Passing laws that recognize the legal and economic needs of some races over the needs of others?

Just look at each of these five bullet points listed above and ask yourself which one will bring America more unity? I strangely find myself very sorry to inform some of my readers that it is absolutely delusional for a thinking person to actually believe that by making a country more diverse it will be stronger and more unified. Does not strength come from unity? Does not weakness come from division? If a people from one country are unified will they be stronger than a people from another country who are diversely divided? I maintain that the social engineering in this country is so complete that many of its citizens actually believe a country can be unified by having multiple races, religions, languages, histories, values and customs. Can we acknowledge the following statements as true?

1. America is a divided nation.
2. Diversity is our strength: Is the slogan of America.
3. Jesus Christ warned in the bible of the destruction of divided kingdoms. (countries)
4. That we as Americans are living in a severely divided country called America.

So who else has figured out America is divided?

1. *Split: A Divided America*: Is a documentary film about partisan divides in American society. It examines the political divide between, Red States/Blue States; Conservatives/Liberals; Republicans/Democrats; from the perspective of cultural factors like religion, urbanization, race, wealth, the modern media, contemporary campaigning strategies, and the deterioration of civil discourse in our political experience.

2. The *BBC,* reports on February 22, 2016: U.S. Election 2016: Divided nation split into more like alien tribes than rival political parties. That's how the Pew Research Center describes how the two sides in an increasingly divided America see each other. They can't stand the other sides viewpoint. The BBC's Franz Strasser looks at the *"demographic trends"* that have made the U.S. Increasingly divided.
3. The *L.A. Times*, May 31, 2016, article titled: President Obama's inability to integrate a divided America.

And on and on it goes. Just do a google search on articles about divided America and prepare to get avalanched. To put this all in a combined biblical perspective, lets look at Gods actions in Genesis 11, and Jesus's warning in Matthew 12.

1. God saw and did not approve of what the people on earth did when they were one with the same language.
2. God separated the people and changed their language thus creating the first racial nation states.
3. Today people are migrating from their original God created nation states and once again coming together as one in multicultural nations.
4. These multicultural nations are producing so much racial, social, religious, and economic division, that the warning by Christ in Matthew 12:25, is being ignored and now the concept of a divided nation is being promoted by governments as a strength.

Does the Christian today believe that God will once again judge todays multicultural nations as He did in Genesis 11? Are we to suffer the destructive fate Christ warned us about in Matthew 12, regarding a divided kingdom? Is the modern multicultural Christian in America even concerned about the historic actions of God and the revelations by Jesus as it relates to this elitist social experiment of multiculturalism in America today?

~ Is God a multiculturalist? ~

If the good Lord expressed His disapproval of the original biblical multicultural nation in Genesis 11, what gives anyone the impression that He has changed His mind about it today? Last I heard God was not the type to be changing with the times to suit His creations opinion of Him.

Old Testament: Malachi 3:6, *For I am the LORD, I change not;*

New Testament: James 1:17, *Every good gift and every perfect gift is from above, and cometh down from the Father of lights, with whom is no variableness, neither shadow of turning.*

What about Gods son Jesus? Is He anything like that living constitution that seems to change with every mood the elitist entertains during any given day?

New Testament: Hebrews 13:8, *Jesus Christ the same yesterday, and today, and for ever.*

So can it be said that the God of Genesis who took corrective action against the original multicultural nation has informed His creations that He does not change? If one follows that logic then one should assume that if man decides to make another multicultural nation in the future, this unchangeable God will be just as displeased as the last time. Okay time to pull out that famous American Whopper mentality of "have it your way" and "its all about me" attitude with the question: Will God consider changing His mind about multicultural nations for the sake of the modern Christians feelings of brotherly love today?

Old Testament: Deuteronomy 10:7, *For the LORD your God is God of gods, and Lord of lords, a great God, a mighty, and a terrible, which regardeth not persons, nor taketh reward:*

New Testament: Acts 10:34, *Then Peter opened his mouth, and said, Of a truth I perceive that God is no respecter of persons:*

So God agrees with Himself from the Old Testament all the way to the new one. He just is not going to respect His creations opinions no matter how modern they think they are and he really cares less if they don't like it. One should come to the conclusion that God created the original nation state by His act of relocating people of particular races to His chosen locations, thus enabling them to form organic tribes which some eventually developed into homogeneous nations by racial default because of Gods judgment of separation. So, since it was God who created the original nations for the various races and ethnic peoples of the world, is it not logical to believe He wanted people to live in the racial nation state? It should be understood by the discerning Christian then that Gods actions in Genesis 11, is in direct conflict with mans actions today as man once again comes together as one in the multicultural nations of today.

Is God an egalitarian? Does God agree with todays elitists that all peoples are created equal? Not really. Look no further than in 1 Samuel, to see what the mighty Lord thinks about some people.

1 Samuel 15:3, *Now go and smite Am'alek, and utterly destroy all that they have, and spare them not; but slay both man and woman, infant and suckling, ox and sheep, camel and ass.*

I believe that ordering the "ancient Israelites" to erase an entire people off the face of the earth by mass genocidal slaughter tells us God by His very own words and actions is not an egalitarian or a multiculturalist. No thinking person can say God loved or even liked the Amalekites and its a safe bet they weren't viewed as equals to the "ancient Israelites" in Gods mind. Does God place some people above others? Of course He does.

Exodus 19:5, *Now therefore, if ye will obey my voice indeed, and keep my covenant, then ye shall be a peculiar treasure unto me above all people: for all the earth is mine*: 6, *and ye shall be unto me a kingdom of priests, and a holy nation.*

Deuteronomy 7:6, *For thou art a holy people unto the LORD thy God: the LORD thy God hath chosen thee to be a special people unto himself, above all people that are upon the face of the earth.*

1 Peter 2:9, *But ye are a chosen generation, a royal priesthood, a holy nation, a peculiar people;that ye should show forth the praises of him who hath called you out of darkness into his marvelous light:*

Well there He goes again. Treating some people better than others. Playing favorites and sometimes downright demanding the annihilation of others. Don't run for cover under some New Testament covenant love theology on this one. 1 Peter 2:9 provides an unbroken chain from the OT to the NT of Gods words and thoughts regarding who He considers above and who He considers below. Now compare these scriptures to the current egalitarian ideology of the elites telling us all people are the same and equal. Do you see the ideological dichotomy between God and the elite multiculturalist? Would todays egalitarian agree with Gods commandment to ancient Israelites to destroy every man, women, and child, of the Amalekites? Do you think todays brotherly love Christian would agree with that same historic commandment by God?

As the churches of today promote racial integration under the false theological umbrella of: "We are all brothers in Christ", is there any reason we should be paying attention to what God really says about the people of the world dwelling together as brothers in Christ?

Jerimiah 31:31,

*Behold, the days come, saith the LORD, that **I will make a new covenant with the house of Israel, and with the house of Judah**: 32, not according to the covenant that I made with their fathers, in the day that I took them by the hand to bring them out of the land of Egypt; which my covenant they brake, although I was a husband unto them, saith the LORD: 33, but this shall be the covenant that I will make with the house of Israel; After those days, saith the LORD, **I will put my law in their inward parts, and write it in their hearts;** and will be their God, and they shall be my people. 34, **And they shall teach no more every man his neighbor, and every man his brother....***

Ah cries the modern love Christian. That is the Old Testament. Not applicable to our New Testament love covenant of today. Okay Mr. Modern, one look forward into the New Testament and if you are actually looking you will find this.

Hebrews 8:8, *For finding fault with them, he saith, Behold, the days come, saith the Lord, when **I will make a new covenant with the house of Israel and with the house of Judah**: 9, not according to the covenant that I made with their fathers, in the day when I took them by the hand to lead them out of the land of Egypt; because they continued not in my covenant, and I regarded them not, saith the Lord. 10, For this is the covenant that I will make with the house of Israel after those days, saith the Lord; **I will put my laws into their mind, and write them in their hearts**: and I will be to them a God, and they shall be to me a people:* 11, **and they shall not teach every man his neighbor, and every man his** brother....

As we can see this is a future covenant which has spanned the millennia and has not been fulfilled yet by God because according to the modern multicultural church of today "we are all brothers in Christ." This covenant was introduced in the OT in Jeremiah and as you can see, word for word re-introduced in the NT Hebrews after Christ has passed. Seems to me for thousands of years God is not too impressed with His people being neighbors with foreigners and them calling everyone their brothers, as He is still waiting to give them this covenant. I feel another AHA moment coming on from the love Christian. *"This covenant is for the ancient tribes of Israel only"* he might say. Well wasn't the Ten Commandments given only to the ancient tribes of Israel also? Using that kind of logic the Christian is going to have to throw out just about every page of Gods theology since now nothing biblical applies to himself. Christ Himself said He came for the tribes of (ancient) Israel only so are you going to X out all His teachings too Mr. Modern Christian? You can look at this scripture anyway you wish to but the words of God remain the same. God does not want His people being neighbors with foreigners and calling everyone their brother and He said it in the OT and in case you are still confused He repeated it in the New Testament.

~ Was Jesus ever a multiculturalist? ~

I guess the next big question is did Jesus come to minister to the world? Was He that guy who reached out to all peoples of the world as some of your Televangelists claim He did? For those paying attention Jesus Himself tells us He was not that guy at all. In fact He didn't show much interest for anyone outside His chosen tribes of Judah and Israel. Here again in Matthew 10, Jesus commanded His apostles on whom they must minister to.

10:5, *These twelve Jesus sent forth, and commanded them, saying, Go not into the way of the Gentiles, and into any city of the Samaritans enter ye not: 6, but go rather to the lost sheep of the house of Israel.*

Jesus is not only telling us who He is interested in but He also is telling us who He is NOT interested in. If one is thinking this is some obscure passage that can be interpreted differently against the weight of other scripture you would be wrong. Jesus again takes the time to inform the Christian bible believer in Matthew 15, He is come for only the ancient tribes of Israel.

15:24, *But he answered and said, I am not sent but unto the lost sheep of the house of Israel.*

Jesus makes it plain for all to see that His divine mission was to minister only to the "lost" tribes of Israel, period! This is not tricky. In fact Jesus sometimes referred to non-Israelites in some very unattractive ways when in Matthew 15, He called one woman a dog and everyone remotely like her a dog, while others He called pigs.

15:26, *But he answered and said, It is not meet to take the children's bread, and to cast it to dogs.*

Understand that Jesus did not even want to talk to this non-Israelite women who was pleading for Jesus to help her daughter. Only after she worshiped Him and admitted she was a dog did He heal her daughter. Does re-considering Jesus's words compromise the love image of Christ the modern church of today worships? Just who are these churches of today worshiping? The real Christ or a perceived love image of the Son of God? Jesus again makes it clear that His ministry is special and meant only for His tribes in Matthew 7.

7:6, *Give not that which is holy unto the dogs, neither cast ye your pearls before swine, lest they trample them under their feet, and turn again and rend you.*

I don't want to be accused of having a Joel Osteen moment here but you really need to understand that when Jesus said something He meant it. Then we find in the book of John 17, Jesus is separating the world from His chosen people, ancient Israel.

17:9, *I pray for them: I pray not for the world, but for them which thou hast given me; for they are thine.*

Here Jesus is once again telling all who have ears to hear it is His apostles of His tribes who is important to Him. So lets put this all together and decide if Jesus sounds like a multiculturalist.

1. Jesus said He was sent only the the tribes of Israel.
2. Jesus instructs His apostles not to give His gospel to non-Israelites.
3. Jesus is on record to have called non-Iraelites dogs, pigs, serpents, and wolves.
4. Jesus in His final days prayed for the apostles of His tribes and not for the world.

Now do any of Jesus's actions sound multicultural? Does He give any impression that His time here on earth was to be spent with all the peoples of the world? It should be clear that Jesus was exclusive with His ministry. No foreigners allowed. If Jesus was a multiculturalist then why didn't He tell us He was sent to the world? Why did His actions prove He treated non-Israelites unequally to Israelites? Doesn't sound very egalitarian at all does it?

It is this authors opinion that many of todays priests and preachers are doing their level best to ignore this important subject on racial separation. They might choose to ignore Gods will in Genesis 11, because they have been successfully socially engineered by Americas pop culture and the government to reject the idea that God separated the races of the world. They might believe that the OT is just an historical record of an ancient people who once roamed the world, therefore it has no theological relevance to todays modern NT Christian. These same men of God might purposely ignore Genesis 11, because they are afraid they might be labeled as some kind of an anti-multicultural racist. Or they may side step the true meaning of the story of the Tower of Babel because they believe that God today is this big fuzzy perpetually happy guy upstairs that just loves everybody all the time no matter what and really does want you to have that new car. You will hear these types of priests and preachers say that we as the modern Christian must love God, but today this new theology of love seems to have replaced the commandment of "Fear God." I am not saying one must not love God but false is the preacher man who makes the claim that God is all about love. Look no further than in Matthew 10.

10:28, *And fear not them which kill the body, but are not able to kill the soul: but rather fear him which is able to destroy both soul and body in hell.*

Can it get any clearer than here in 2nd Corinthians 7?

7:1, *Having therefore these promises, dearly beloved, let us cleanse ourselves from all filthiness of the flesh and spirit, perfecting holiness in the fear of God.*

There are at least twenty scriptures in the New Testament talking about continuing the Old Testament commandment of fearing God. The evidence is clear for those who have eyes to see that the NT agrees with the OT as it relates to Proverbs.

1:7, *The fear of the LORD is the beginning of knowledge: but fools despise wisdom and instruction*

But where do fools wonder?

Proverbs 21:16, *The man that wandereth out of the way of understanding shall remain in the congregation of the dead.*

Just what is this "fear" God is talking about? Is He saying you should walk around all hunched over wondering if He will strike you dead on any given day? No, not that kind of fear. Let me give you an analogy of what God means by fearing Him.

> *"Say you and your little boy are out in the front yard one summer day. You are washing the car and he is playing. Junior suddenly sees a nice shiny toy across the street. Junior being three years old and walking wants that toy. Being a toddler he doesn't understand that there are cars passing by and cannot see the danger of the street at this age. Junior begins to walk towards the street in anticipation of securing the toy across it. You being the watchful parent raise your voice and say "stop now!" Junior turns and looks at you. It is at this time "if" you have been the type of parent to raise your child in the Godly manner by spanking him when naughty, he will think, "father has a heavy swat in that hand and that scares me, maybe he knows something I don't. I better stop right here." Thus raising your child to fear you can save his life or save him from injury. But! If you raised your child with love and no fear of the pain of spankings, then when you say, "stop now!" Junior will look at you and think, "my father loves me no matter what I do. There is nothing to fear about him. I just might go ahead and cross the street to get that toy." Therefore he will place himself in danger of the oncoming cars. Thus, since junior has no fear of father what is to stop him from doing what he wants to do? "*

Now just insert you as an adult into the role of the toddler, and the father of this analogy into the role of God. We are like a toddler compared to Gods ultimate wisdom. God sees the big picture and we many times do not. This is why we must pray for His guidance. God sometimes places us in a strange or even a fearful situation we don't understand. It is in these times we must trust Him *and be fearful NOT to do His will*. This is the fear we must have. It is also in these times we must understand we are on His time clock and not ours. Things will happen the way He wants them to and when He wants them to by us fearing God, having patience and waiting on the Lord.

Isn't it true that the typical pop culture preacher of today will tell you God loves everyone right? God is love. But did God really say He loved everyone? Well step back and take another look at the word of God minus the perverted pop culture of love theology today.

Malachi 1:2, ...*Was not Esau Jacob's brother? saith the LORD: yet I loved Jacob*, 3, *and I hated Esau*....

How does this statement fly in the face of the preacher mans "God loves us all" sermons of today? Now is Gods statement a misquote or a theological typo? For the New Testament crowd I submit the following on how God shows us yet again He does not change.

Romans 9:13, *As it is written, Jacob have I loved, but Esau have I hated.*

God does hate and He's not afraid to tell you that in either Testament. So this is my point. While I truly believe one must love God with all his heart and soul, that will not change the reality that:

1. You must still fear God.
2. God and Jesus by their own scriptural words and actions are not multiculturalists.

God and Jesus have made it known to all they they hate, disapprove of, and even have desired the death of certain peoples. The bible believing Christian knows that God created different kinds of people for His earth. But after His little creations did something really naughty He separated them by race during the judgment on the Tower of Babel. How do I know He separated them by race? Because He told us He also changed the languages of the people. That should give us a clue that since historically we found all Black Africans in Africa speaking African languages, and all Asians were in Asia speaking Asian languages, as Whites were historically in Europe, and Indians were in the Americas speaking their own dialects of their languages. There is no record of an ancient Japanese person speaking Irish Gaelic, nor an ancient Britain speaking Swahili. Secular history agrees with God. Man was as much historically as biblically separated by race and placed in separate geographical locations.

So take a good look around and ask yourself these four questions:

1. Do you live in a multicultural country?
2. Do you support or promote multiculturalism in America?
3. Do you believe you as a Christian have the authority to undue Gods judgment in Genesis 11?
4. Was Jesus talking about your country when He said a divided kingdom is brought to destruction?

The Tower of Babel judgment by God marked the origins of all nations on earth. For the Christian to defy the will of God by once again coming together as one in multicultural countries is to "knowingly" invite the wrath of Gods judgment.

FIRST PRINCIPLES AND A RETURN TO THE CENTER OF YOUR CULTURE

It has been said there are two ways to hold together the inherently unstable multicultural nation. Money and force. When there is plenty of money to throw around all seems to go pretty well doesn't it? College scholarships abound, plenty of social programs to invent and fund, and building projects everywhere that continually feed the something for nothing economy. But the problem with an economic system that depends upon a massive infusion of monetary stimulus to keep it afloat is that this money for all the happy programs usually is not real money. Meaning it borrowed. Borrowed money means debt. A growing debt unpaid year after year equals more debt. Endless debt eventually will result in some sort of default. Kind of like pushing a snowball downhill. The next logical question is how long can the party last? Unfortunately not forever. Sooner or later the lender comes a calling and no more can you produce one credit card to pay for another. A nation spoon fed on debt is like a junkie that gets free drugs. He gets used to it real quick and after a while he even begins to expect the free ride will never end. But when it does end like all free rides must, so ends the niceties associated with it.

And here is my premise,

> *The inherently unstable multicultural nation will always fall into decline for either economic reasons or social reasons and many times due to a combination*

> of both. When that happens the multicultural nation tends to degenerate into racial violence as societal norms break down due to the competition of (now) scarce resources. While a true organic nation has the advantage of racial and cultural commonalities to assist the people in pulling together during times of stress and adversity, kind of like a family does, the multicultural nation having divided cultural characteristics tends to violently balkanize.

Why is this a truism? Because the elite social experiment called the multicultural nation can never be a true nation in the first place because it wasn't formed by the natural process of a consenting common people from a common geographical origin. For the most part the organic nation by its very creation will avoid the many cultural pitfalls, social tripwires, and economic stumbling blocks, that the multicultural nation literally must sabotage itself with just to even exist.

~ Empires and non-Empires ~

Here is the most ignored and avoided word in the elite multiculturalists vocabulary. Balkanization. They have heard of it, they know what it is, and they will do their level best to shovel dirt on it in hopes of burying it. But somehow balkanizations historical reflection will still gaze into the eyes of the elitist with a familiarity that can only reveal a constant reminder of failure for those who walk down the road to this kind of instability. Yes it is the elites who ignore history in their quest for a world empire that extends beyond the natural nation state.

But empires are great aren't they? Never met one that stuck around though. Is not history replete with the downfall of empires? From Babylon to Britain, all the worlds empires ended up crumbling under their own greedy obese weight and pride didn't they? One mirror

America does not want to hold up in front of its face is one that has the Roman empire in it. From spreading fear and awe across the Mediterranean for economic tribute, to eventually being taken over by what the Romans considered to be barbarians in a multicultural disaster. But we Americans are modern aren't we? History just does not apply to us. Why everyone knows we are the exception to all historical rules. Then there was that Turkish Ottoman empire that eventually ended up being called the "sick man" of Europe. Lets not forget that British empire that stretched itself as well as its currency to a point of no return. Then there is that non-empire. You know. The one that wasn't, but now is, but never claims to be, empire called America. The empire of the United States has troops in over 135 nations. This means that it has a military presence in around 70% of the worlds countries. The average American probably couldn't locate half of these countries on a map. The U.S. non-empire global foot print today is an empire that Alexander the Great, Genghis Khan, and King George V, would be envious of.

So where are all these historical empires today? The only place you will find them is in your history books. Now that odd non-empire is still hanging around isn't it? We know it's an empire but just cannot mouth the words. We know that this non-empire is beginning to show signs of being a sick man. We also know that it is quickly running out of money so it must now depend upon some type of computer to create money to pay its bills don't we? But not to worry, the printing presses are in good order and this non-empire is about to be saved by something called *"change we can believe in."* So far the only change we have witnessed is evidenced by President Obama's remarkable ability to keep these money creating computers operating at full speed without breaking down. But can we keep printing enough money to keep our country from eventually economically imploding? The Liberal of the day says *"yes we can."* But can we? This political stumble bum of a country called America is so big and clumsy it cannot even fiscally run a post office.

Can America run its government? As reported by: http://www.usgovernmentdebt.us/: At the end of FY 2016, the total government debt in the United States including Federal, State, and Local, is expected to be $22.4 trillion. (NOTE: zoom forward to 2023 and that number now is $31 trillion)

Can America run its retirement programs? *Naturalnews.com* reports on November 17, 2015, in an article titled: US Govt admits Social Security is going bankrupt; warns public should be given adequate time to prepare for the collapse.

Can America educate its children? *Great Schools* reports: The United States may be a superpower but in education we lag behind. Students in the United States on the world stage performed near the middle of the pack. On average 16 other industrialized countries scored above the United States in science and 23 scored above the U.S. in math. http://www.greatschools.org/gk/articles/u-s-students-compare/

Can America run its medical programs? As reported by Senator *John Barrasso*, Chairman, in 2013: http://www.rpc.senate.gov/policy-papers/medicare-remains-on-fast-track-to-bankruptcy-

Can America control its borders? Think we know that answer already.

Can America produce successful citizens? The *Washington Post* reports on July 7, 2015, the U.S. locks people up at a higher rate than any other country. "It's a stark fact that the United States has less than 5% of the worlds population, yet we have almost 25% of the worlds total prison population."

Which country is the most medicated in the world? *Webmarks* Online reports on February 10, 2014, that the United States for sure and by far is the most medicated country in the world.

How do Americans rate their own country? The *World Happiness Report* 2016, is a measure of happiness published by the United Nations Sustainable Development Solutions Network. The U.S. people scored 13th on the international level with a red arrow pointing down. We cannot even make the top ten for happiness in the land of the free(?) and the home of the.....richest.

I wonder if those participating in the happiness poll took their medications first before they voted? So is it odd to say this country can no longer sustain itself economically and cannot govern "we the people" effectively anymore? I understand the need for many Americans to adopt the social attitude of "optimism bias" which probably is acquired by wearing out at least two pairs of rose colored glasses a year, but sooner or later ya'll gonna catch a right cross to the chin from Mr. Reality.

~ It's all about the tribe and it has always been ~

When economic times are good the liberal ideology of easy money is easy to promote. But when times get tough people tend to naturally start getting a little conservative in their thinking and in their actions. People begin to remove those rose colored glasses handed out by the liberal progressives and start to focus. When this happens those once trusty fashionable cliche's like "diversity is our strength" will quickly get court martialed to the no longer applicable file and get replaced with something called: Tribal Re-integration, or, sticking with one's own. Why is this true? To use an example: In tough economic times if an employed Black man knows there is only one job available at the local factory he will out of pure natural instinct want an unemployed member of his family to have it and he will act on that common sense. The same goes for the White man, etc. To not act on ones own survival instincts in times of adversity is to deny ones own reason for existence. Further, is it not true that most Blacks still marry in their own race as most other races do? The reason why in times of adversity people will naturally split along racial lines and tribal re-integrate is because of that marriage percentage. The American family group is still usually leaning towards homogeneous. We also know most neighborhoods tend to lean on the homogeneous side to varying degrees, some more than others. We know that racial demographics of a neighborhood is a strong criteria for home buyers. It's this natural process of satisfying the individuals intimate social well being of desiring to live among ones own that is in direct conflict with the elite multiculturalists ideology and world strategy.

Today you would be hard pressed to find a White man that would want to take a stroll in a Black neighborhood at night. He'd probably even think more than once about it during the day time. This type of thinking probably can be applied to the Mexican neighborhood as well. To be fair, there have been some incidents of Blacks venturing into the wrong White neighborhood and falling into unfortunate circumstances. It's true that some neighborhoods in America practice a violent form of racism if the wrong skin job saunters into it. A Jewish co-worker once told me that when the sun went down in his old neighborhood in New York, a group of Jewish men would patrol the streets looking to forcibly relocate people they considered racial undesirables. If racial discrimination is happening today at these levels imagine how it will be if poop hits the fan blades. I can foretell that the promoters of the glories of multiculturalism will see their social experiment quickly fall apart as survival instincts take over and self preservation becomes the primary goal of the people.

In Americas past there have been riots caused by the beating of a Black man by the police. There have been riots in Europe and South America over something as silly as a soccer game as well in America over a football game. There have been food riots and water riots, but when a people of a certain race come to a concurring conclusion that they have been racially violated and feel they have no other recourse than to strike out at someone or some entity then death comes swiftly and in multiples. In the 1965 Watts race riots in Los Angeles, the victim count was 34 dead and 1000 injured. In the 1967 Newark, New Jersey riots, 26 died and 1500 were injured followed by 10 million dollars worth of damage. Just a mere two weeks later after the Jersey riots, a riot in Detroit left 43 dead. In the 1992 race riots in Los

Angeles we saw 54 go down permanently and more than 2000 hospitalized, while 862 buildings were burned to the ground. More recently in Baltimore, civil unrest saw at least 20 police officers injured, at least 250 people arrested, 285 to 350 businesses damaged, 150 vehicles fires, 60 structure fires, and 27 drugstores looted. Hundreds of police and the Maryland Army National Guard were deployed and a state of emergency was declared in the city limits. Then in Fergussen, Missouri more riots in 2015. My point here is in times of adversity these riots will get a lot more lethal. So I say why must we let it go that far?

Some reading this book right now might say, "why this guy has no confidence in the American way." It's not that I don't have any confidence in my fellow countrymen but I do have two advantages when judging people in adverse conditions. First, I have the understanding that during periods of adversity peoples survival instincts will prevail over social norms, and second, I never bought a house in Liberal la la land.

It's not rocket science to understand that we as Americans are not socially integrating within our ever changing demography. The unspoken truth for most of us is that it's very hard for the American citizen to call some new 3rd world immigrant just off the boat who cannot speak one word of English his cultural brother. Now to the globalists our forever racially morphing demography is a cultural positive. When in the process of enlightening you on this subject they will thoughtfully look up to the heavens, squint their eyes, wrinkle their foreheads, and tell you we all belong to the family of man and all cultures are as good and equal to your own. All the while they themselves in their own gated neighborhoods practice that unique dance move called the NIMBY shuffle. You know the one:

> Move it to the left.
> Move it to the right.
> **Not In My Back Yard** and out of my sight.

But voodoo worship, genital mutilation, and killing non-combatants for a chance of acquiring 72 brown eyed chicks with no bedroom experience, tells the average American he just might have a different set of values from many of the new incoming immigrants.

~ Are you still waiting for that leopard to change its spots? ~

Today some people in America still believe we can vote this country out of trouble. You'll see these excited chattel every four years wearing their party hats and blowing their tweety horns for the latest political funsters to be paraded out by the only two political parties we are allowed to have. Year after year, election after election, we as American citizens must suffer through the forever ongoing campaign battles being waged over the coveted seat of some government office somewhere in America. The Democrat will square off with the Republican in usually a very nasty campaign. "Vote for me and I will fight for you" is the clarion call of the candidate. So tell me. Who is this candidate going to fight? Why his fellow Americans of course. You have about a 50% chance of being a candidates target depending on which political party he is in and which one you are not. These elected paragons of virtue will label you either an extreme right wing kook or a limp wristed liberal. They might say that you belong to that soft mushy crowd in the center called moderates, or they may find out that you are the dreaded independent. Whatever the nonsense that is falling out of the teeth of these candidates mouths, we as Americans not only have to put up with this phoniness but to add insult to injury we usually end up paying for these elections by way of taxes and campaign donations.

To increase our misery just pick up any newspaper or click on any internet news site and you'll soon find yourself drowning in a political landslide of mudslinging newsmen. Turn on the nightly news and you'll see newsmen and newswomen talking at you, talking over you, but never failing to tell you how rotten those liberals are or how mean those conservatives are. Can you ever imagine a day when conservative Sean Hannity will have his political views reconstructed by a liberal such as Rachael Maddow? Can you imagine in your wildest dreams Hillary Clinton ever saying, "gosh darn it, Pat Buchanan was right all along about illegal immigration!" Will Chuck Shumer ever tell us we as Americans have the right to own any gun we wish to? Anyone volunteering to hold their breath? The next question screaming to be answered is why should a liberal such as ole tingle britches Chris Matthews be required to change his political views for my personal enjoyment? If Chris wants to be a liberal then why should I as a conservative feel it is my duty to right his head? I would think it would be common knowledge by now that the liberals and conservatives are never going to find any common ground. For a conservative to change to a liberal he would have to lose a good chunk of his religion. For a liberal to change to a conservative he would have to lose all his religion because the liberal ideology is the religion of the liberal. It should be understood that these two ideologies in America have and will be in conflict with each other forever.

The basic ideology of the conservative is: Lower taxes, less government, strong military, and traditional family values. The basic ideology of the liberal is the opposite. What this tells the thinking individual is that these two competing types of ideologies cannot politically coexist. Caught in the cross-fire of these two warring factions is Main Street America as it is socially, economically, and even theologically, dragged across the left and right of the political spectrum during the election cycle as the candidates battle for their votes. Why must the Christian be forced to accept the gay life style when it goes against his religion? Why must the liberal be forced to accept Christian symbols or religious references in public places when it goes against his religion? Is it healthy for a country to force a large segment of its population to accept and support values and programs that they view as extremely offensive? American middle class voters are forced to dwell in this curious and even damaging political and cultural realm that states:

- The conservatives will fight forever for their agenda.
- The liberals will fight forever for their agenda.
- We as citizens of this country will forever be caught in the cross-fire of their endless war.

Am I the only one in this country that is sick and tired of being a political ping pong ball in the ongoing tournament of Republicans against Democrats? Shouldn't a real country have a set of basic common customs and values that not only unite us but are even a comfort to us? Shouldn't a real country have a relatively common idea on how it sees its future? Shouldn't a real country be able to celebrate its holidays in peace? Several decades ago for those who remember, it used to be that way wasn't it? How this Keystone Cop election cycle usually spins around in this country is when one party wins the Presidency, the winning party is usually in office just long enough to get the voting majority of the nation either sick of their policies or disgusted with their corruption just enough to elect the other party, and then the cycle repeats itself.

Here is a summary of your Presidential triumphs, or maybe scandals, in America starting in 1968.

In comes **Republican** Nixon. After a few years oops, there's a Watergate in the pool which made the Vice President Ford the following Presidential token bump in the rode.

Next was this **Democrat** peanut farmer from Georgia with enough teeth in his face to send Sigourney Weaver running into the arms of an alien. For some reason President Carter decided to blow a hole in the economy and leave some unfortunates in Iran for an unwanted extended visit.

Which, caused a **Republican** by the name of Mr. "A New Beginning" Reagan to be elected. After have an affair with Iran-Contra and legalizing millions of illegal aliens he escaped office relatively still likable.

On Reagans coattails and out of the bush came a Bush. He was a **Republican** who had trouble figuring out he was elected to work for America. He was able to save his son from an S & L scandal by way of making America pay for it.

Next was a **Democrat** named Clinton who made a science out of telling us which women he didn't sleep with. But thanks to Yodas doppelganger from Texas he slipped into office for another term.

Then we pulled another **Republican** out of the bush who was also strangely named Bush. After four years and an economic stimulus that would make a Democrat soil himself, we gave him another shot.

Then came **Democrat** Barry Soetoro who changed his name to Obama Hussein, who would have trouble joining an American little league team for lack of proper legal identification. But not to worry because his affordable healthcare program will save the day. The computer costs for Obama Care were only 834 million dollars while spending over 2 billion dollars enrolling all the people in America who didn't want it in the first place.

Ping pong anyone?

~ Libertarians to the rescue ~

Now today some are of the mind to shank both of these political parties and form a new one but have we not walked down this road before? Witness the rise of the Libertarian party. No, really, witness it. This crew has been in the game or at least watching the game since 1971. But zoom forward and not one seat in the U.S. Senate or House was sat on by a butt owned by a libertarian until 2016. In fact, this party has never had anyone of their candidates elected in the Senate or House until two Republicans defected to that party in that same year. How about that Reform Party founded in 1995 by Ross the Boss Perot from Texas? Who can forget Perot's stellar performance at the 1996 debates? Oh, that's right, silly me. I forgot that the Reform Party candidate was not allowed to participate in the national televised Presidential debates that year. For some reason Ross as an Independent candidate was allowed to participate in the 1992 debates but was x'd out in 1996 by the FEC (Federal Election Committee). So after splitting the conservative votes twice to secure the election of democrat Bill Clinton to the Presidency, Ross just up and left. With the exit of Perot, conservative icon Pat Buchanan took over the reins of the Reform Party, saddled it up and made a dash for the Presidency in 2000. As before the Reform Party candidate was not welcomed by Republicans or the Democrats in the national televised debates. No share? The Reform Party is still alive and last I heard it is fairing about as well in DC as the Libertarian Party is.

So what happened to the Tea Party? Should we form yet another political party to save the day? Sometimes the history of political 3rd parties in America can be compared to an old "Threes Company" re-run. It's gonna be just as good as the last time you saw it. What should be clear by now is this country has been set up to be serviced by a two party political system. These two parties controlling the FEC have a lot of motivation NOT to divide the game into thirds. Today there are over twenty political parties in the U.S. They come with names such as the Constitution Party, the Green Party, to even a New Black Panther Party. So in the world of American Politics what does one really hope to accomplish by forming yet another party? Either way let history be the judge of the historical success of 3rd parties here on this turf.

~ Divide us by Diversity ~

So if some type of national adversity strikes the nation and our government cannot supply the public with the financial glue to hold this multicultural country together will the White American rush into South Central Los Angeles to help the Mexican population with a portion of his saved food? Will the Black American rush into the Eastern Kentucky hills to share his lunch with those folks? Will the crew from China Town call the Appalachian country folk to come down from the mountain and share their survival supplies? Will we Americans of different races come together and unite in our time of need as a single national brotherhood? Short answer. We won't. Why? Since the 1960's we were not supposed to be united as Americans. How can I say that? Is not the slogan of America now "diversity is our strength"? Diversity and united are two different words with two different meanings. "United" means coming together as one. But doesn't "diverse" mean different? Are we not encouraged by our government to be diverse by celebrating multicultural holidays like Cinco de Mayo and events like Black History Month, Asian Week, and even Gay Pride? Does not our government fund programs like the EEOC and Civil Rights laws that work to ensure our diversity stays strong? The different races and ethnic peoples in America have become more galvanized in their unique cultures and racial differences because they have not had to assimilate into the original mainstream American culture. Remember, we are a political salad bowl and not a melting pot anymore. Don't forget, this country doesn't even call its people Americans anymore. Is it not true we are called: African Americans, Mexican Americans, or even Latinos, as well as Asian Americans, and Native Americans? Have we become the hyphenated country? It should be common knowledge that anything divided, diverse, or diluted, loses its full strength from its original whole. But hey, that's only chemistry right? Well let's look at this statement "diversity is our strength" a little closer and judge for yourself how this elitist diversity theory fails on its own merits.

Is diversity a strength in this example?

- Say you have two different work crews, both with 10 men who are going to build a house. One crew has 2 Haitians, 2 Mexicans, and 1 Korean, who don't speak English and 5 who only speak English. The other crew all speak English. Who will have a much easier time building the house better, quicker, and more economically?
Is diversity a strength in this example?
- Say we have two classrooms in Texas. One that is filled with mostly White students and the other mostly filled with Mexican American students. The history subject is the Texas story of the Alamo. Which class will the teacher have an easier time teaching the about the heroic efforts of Davey Crockett and Jim Bowie?
Is diversity a strength in this example?
- If you place 3 soccer players and 2 volley ball players on one baseball teams starting roster and have them play another team with a full roster of baseball players, will not the baseball ball team with a full roster of baseball players win a game between the two?

The point here is every time you begin mixing and dividing the original whole of anything it changes that whole to a point of either it no longer is what it was, or it is not as effective as it originally was intended to be.

Isn't it true that most people want to belong to someone and some place? It is the opinion of this author that most people want to be able to walk downtown in their city and feel that they are a part of the people they see there. To be able to see a stranger and feel they share many values and commonalities without even knowing that person. This creates a natural sense of belonging. This is the basic human need that is in the cross-hairs of the promoters of multiculturalism. These multiculturalists will tell you that an official unifying language does not matter. They will tell you that it doesn't matter what religion you are. That it doesn't matter if you don't share a set of common values with your neighbors, or that your sexual orientation doesn't matter when using a bathroom. Multiculturalism is a phony ideology that these elitists invented to prosecute their divide and conquer New World Order agenda.

Why should the Christian, be they Black, White, or whatever race have to take the chance of being caught in another judgment by God because their government forces them to live in a multicultural country? For those who understand, this forced subjugation not only goes against our beliefs but it impacts our very sense of survival. Just maybe it's time for a relocation. This politically clumsy ox of a country is big enough to divide up into several countries isn't it? Why not volunteer to balkanize freely under our own terms? Or why not take a boat ride to an island somewhere and set up a new nation there? I am not silly enough to think every Christian is just going to up and move to a new country but these ideas must be introduced for all to consider before the possibility of a future event forces balkanization in a non-peaceful manner. If God wishes the Christian to relocate from the multicultural nation then maybe it's time to ask for His blessing on such an endeavor.

~ Democracy, the divisive failure of a Nation ~

So can we even believe that our type of democratic government can eventually fix the problems that besiege this nation today? It is a true statement that Democracy by its very nature must be divisive. The reality is it cannot exist without division. Why? First, whoever heard of a Democratic country with just one political party? Are not political parties always in competition with each other for control of a country? As said before, how many politicians have you heard say they will fight for you? That of course means they must fight their own countrymen for you if you are their supporting voter. The voter himself is also against other voters who are on the opposite side of an election or an issue. So can we agree that political parties are divisive? Simply put, Democracy splits the people into divisive factions creating hostility as they now view their fellow citizens as potential adversaries at best and enemies at worst as they battle for resources, thus pushing the primary goal of a nation towards materialism. Is this any way to nurture and secure a healthy vision of a country's future? But Democracy loving Americans want to have the power to vote for their President don't they? Ever heard of the Electoral College?

The Electoral College consists of 538 electors. A majority of 270 electoral votes is required to elect the President. You help choose your states electors when you vote for a President *because when you vote for your candidate you are actually voting for your candidates electors.*

Wikipedia delves into this Electoral College a little deeper. "The United States Electoral College is the institution that elects the President and the Vice President of the United States every four years. **Citizens of the United States do not directly elect the president or the vice president**; instead these voters directly elect designated intermediaries called "electors" who *almost always* have pledged to vote for particular presidential and vice presidential candidates (though unpledged electors are possible) and who are themselves selected according to the particular laws of each state."

So how much did those party hats and tweety horns cost you Mr. President non-voter? Did you catch the *Wikipedia* part that said "almost always"? This "almost always" thing came into play when four Presidents in the history of this country were not elected by the popular vote of the people.

- In 1824 John Quincy Adams was elected president despite not winning either the popular vote or the electoral vote. Andrew Jackson was the winner in both categories.

- In 1876 Rutherford B. Hayes won the election by a margin of one electoral vote, but he lost the popular vote by more than 250,000 ballots to Samual J. Tilden.
- In 1888 Benjamin Harrison received 233 electoral votes to Grover Clevelands 168, winning the presidency. But Harrison lost the popular vote by more then 90,000 votes.
- In 2000 George W. Bush was declared the winner of the general election and became the 43rd President but he didn't win the popular vote either. Al Gore holds that distinction garnering about 540,000 more votes than Bush. However, Bush won the electoral vote, 271 to 266.
- So 2020 arrives and some American voters have figured out that using Chinese communist voting machines, extending the election process for weeks, late night bundle deliveries at voting precincts, politicians with no questions, and an uninterested Supreme Court, guarantees pre-chosen winners in elections that no one can believe in anymore.

Is it true what they say about democracies and that they all will eventually fail? Here is a famous quote from a Scot, Alexander Fraser Tytler, Scottish Lawyer and writer, 1770,

> *"A democracy is always temporary in nature; it simply cannot exist as a permanent form of government. A democracy will continue to exist up until the time that the voters discover that they can vote themselves generous gifts from the public treasury. From that moment on, the majority always votes for the candidates who promise the most benefits from the public treasury, with the result that every democracy will finally collapse due to loose fiscal policy"*

Think America is broken today? Funny how many American voters call their candidates political whores, but who keeps voting for them so these same whores can give them goodies? Here is a quote from one of your founders and U.S. President, John Adams. *"Remember, democracy never lasts long. It soon wastes, exhausts, and murders itself. There never was a democracy yet that did not commit suicide."*

Author James Madison of our Constitutional Bill of Rights had this to say about Democracy. *"Democracy is the vilest form of government....democracies have ever been spectacles of turbulence and contention; have ever been found incompatible with personal security or the rights of property; and have in general been as short in their lives as they have been violent in their deaths."*

Seems a few of our founders don't think your future sounds very promising. What the main problem with democracy is, is that it keeps you in a state of comatose between election cycles. Then every two and mainly four years the people wake up and vote for the next group of candidates and if their candidate doesn't win, democracy tells them to go back to bed and try again later. What this form of government really does is keep the charade going as Americans continue think their vote will matter....next time. But with two entrenched political parties keeping out other competing political parties, that voter idea of next time never comes. Just ask any true conservative if supporting Newt Gingrich's Republican Revolution of 1994 spearheaded by the "Contract with America" changed anything. Zoom forward and how about that Republican political landslide in 2010 with the GOP capturing the House. The voters sent a strong message of discontent to President Obama and his administrations policies. Did the country reverse itself and move right? Am I the only one who is having trouble figuring out where all those 2010 voters disappeared to in the 2012 Presidential election? I would like to ask the Christian a question. Has this country ever reversed its moral decline when a Republican President was in office? What needs to be finally understood by the

American voter is: You cannot vote your way out of something you never voted yourself in to. Meaning, we all know now that using communist Chinese voting machines run by democrats and rhino republicans means our elections can only leave us with a corrupt outcome.

The Social Order of a country is divided into three distinct layers.

1. Top Layer: Elites, Politicians, and Corporate leaders. The rule makers.
2. Middle Layer: Military, Law Enforcement. The enforcers of the rules made by the Top Layer.
3. Bottom Layer: The Citizens of the country. The People.

The Top Layer and the Middle Layer are financially supported by, and understood to be in the service of the Bottom Layer. The only way the Top Layer can tyrannize the Bottom Layer is if the Middle Layer enforces their tyranny.

So who invented this thing called Democracy and who did they invent it for? It was Pagan Greece that invented this form of government around 500 BC for the Pagan Greeks. Even though Pagan Rome is classified as a Republic and not a democracy per se, its history helped preserve the concept of democracy over the centuries. We have all heard of that famous Roman Senate. So today what makes Christians think a government invented by Pagans for Pagans is the best form of government for them? Ever heard of ancient Israel electing a President? Did Moses ever mention any political parties or democracy? Seems democracy is not very biblical at all. Seems to me every time a Pagan or someone of a different religion is offended by a Christian symbol in public view our own form of pagan democratic government wastes no time removing it. So we should know America got its form of government from Pagan Greece and Pagan Rome but is there any other pagan symbology in the American government? Look no further than who's standing on top of the U.S. State Capitol building. A cross? A statue of Jesus? Statue of Moses? Nope. How about the Pagan Goddess Athena masquerading as the "Statue of Freedom." That's right. That's her helmet. The twelve stars surrounding the headdress of this so called Statue of Freedom represents the Zodiac, an ancient Pagan astrological concept.

Thomas Crawford, Statue of Freedom
(U.S. Capitol dome), 1863.
Bronze (cast by Robeert Mills), 234 inches.
Source: Courtesy of the Architect of the Capitol.

And what do we find standing at the entrance of the U.S. Capitol building? A statue of the Roman god Mars.

THE LIVING SIN • 189

Entrance to the U.S. Capitol building   The Pagan God, Mars

Recognize this thing anywhere in Washington DC?

Egyptian obelisk

Washington DC monument obelisk

Yet another image of paganism in the Justice Dept. building. The statue of the Spirit of Justice.

THE LIVING SIN • 191

On April 21, 1787, the Congress of the Confederation of the United States authorized a design for an official copper penny, later referred to as the Fugio cent outfitted with a pagan sun and sundial.

And there is the famous Mercury dime.

Is our paper money as guilty as our coinage? Yes, witness the Pyramid and all seeing eye on U.S. dollar .

THE LIVING SIN • 193

Yet even our military's medals of honor do not escape these Pagan deities. Why doesn't this so called Christian nation have biblical heroes like King David or Joshua on its medals?

U.S. Army Medal of Honor

U.S. Navy Medal of Honor

U.S. Airforce Medal of Honor

How about what NASA names its space ships? From Mercury to Gemini to Apollo, all pagan names.

So where are the statues of Jesus Christ on our government properties? Last I heard Alabama's judicial ethics panel removed Chief Justice Roy Moore from office in 2003 for defying a federal judge's order to remove a Ten Commandments monument from that States Supreme Court building. I find it odd that Christians in America will put up with their government removing from public view all symbols of Christianity but not a peep out of them concerning all the Pagan gods in plain view in this country's capitol city. But if one takes the time to research this subject you will find that Washington DC and America in general is literally saturated with pagan symbology. There are so many everyday items named after demons that Americans should feel like they are on a first-name basis with God's enemies.

Hermes - Hermes bags/purses; Hermes is also the logo of FTD flowers; and **Atlas** - Goodyear tires. Atlas, a book of maps; also Atlas Van Lines, a moving company; many different companies/products named after Atlas. **Apollo** - a car manufactured by Buick; the

Apollo Theater in NYC; and also the Apollo Space Program. **Echo** - a car manufactured by Toyota. **Eos** - a convertible manufactured by Volkswagen. **Orion** - Orion Pictures Corporation. **Nike** - a shoe company. **Saturn** – a brand of car; an award. **Titan** – an insurance company; an outdoor advertising company; an ocean liner; and a movie.

All of the planets (except earth) and many of the astronomical objects have pagan names.
Mercury
Venus
Mars
Jupiter
Saturn
Uranus
Neptune
Pluto

Many other everyday names of products and companies come from pagan mythology including Aurora, Amazon and Ajax, and that's just starting with the letter "A." Christians aren't even supposed to SPEAK the names of pagan gods (demons).
Exodus 23:13,

> *"And in all things that I have said unto you be circumspect: and make no mention of the name of other gods, neither let it be heard out of thy mouth."*

Just maybe this country called America is not really what it claims to be, i.e. "one nation under God." Maybe this country is actually something else.

Seeking prophetic answers we will turn to the biblical book of Revelations. This one book could fill a warehouse of interpretations. What I have found in this book is there is not one but three Babylons. Why three? Because in the chapters 17, 18, 19, we find these Babylons "were and will be" destroyed in three different ways. That can only mean Revelations is telling us there are/were three different Babylons.

Babylon #1: To understand Babylon in revelations you must acquire the discernment that this word "Babylon" is a biblical code word for evil and is presented more than once in the book of Revelations in an out of a sequenced timeline. These three Babylons in Revelations are not to be confused with the ancient Babylon in Mesopotamia, Iraq. This Babylon #1 that is mentioned in revelation chapters 13, 14, 15, 16, 19, is the ancient empire of Rome when under the emperor Nero. In Matthew 24, Jesus tells his apostles of a coming tribulation and after it ends He tells them of is His second coming. This tribulation Jesus is talking about begins in Revelations 13.

- In Rev. 13, the tribulation is now starting and the beast causes all to get the mark on their right hand or forehead.
- In Rev. 14, an angel warns those who worship the beast and receives his mark will drink the wine of the wrath of God.
- In Rev. 15, the warning of the coming of seven plagues.
- In Rev. 16, Gods angels pour out the seven bowls (plagues) of wrath upon the earth. After a great earthquake a great city was split into three parts and the cities of nations fell. At this point Babylon was remembered by God to give her the cup of His fierce wrath.

(Deviation from the timeline) It is important to know at this time that God has not dealt with Babylon #1 yet as the tribulation is well underway. Now the trick here is to understand that whoever put together the bible made an abrupt change at the end of ch.16, and inserted a future prophesy regarding an entity called Mystery Babylon in ch. 17 (**Babylon #2**) then in ch. 18, another future prophesy of an economic Babylon (**Babylon #3**) an altogether different Babylon. Many bible historians make the mistake of claiming Mystery Babylon encompasses chapters 17 & 18. Again, one is a mystery and one is not and they are both destroyed in two different ways.

To continue the story of **Babylon #1** we skip over ch. 17 & 18.

- In Rev. 19, half way down the page the story of **Babylon #1** continues from ch 16, with Christs second coming to conquer the beast, the false prophet, and Nero and his armies. In Rev. 20, Christ has finished the job and Satan is bound for 1000 years. Thus the destruction of **Babylon #1,** which was the empire of ancient Rome which included the beast, the false prophet, and Nero and his armies, was accomplished by Christ and His armies.

Now going back to ch. 17, we find in Revelations a second Babylon.

Babylon #2: Mystery Babylon. This mystery is a prophesy that has been solved by author Dave Hunt in his book: *A woman rides the beast*. This woman is non other than the Catholic Church. Citing this book I will connect the dots of Mystery Babylon that all point to the Catholic Church in Vatican City.

1) Rev. 17:9, *Here is the mind which has wisdom. The seven heads are* **seven mountains** *on which the woman sits,*

The location of Mystery Babylon is built on seven mountains or hills. The Catholic Encyclopedia states: It is within the city of Rome, called the city of seven hills, that entire area of Vatican state proper is now confined.

2) *Rev. 17:1, Then one of the seven angels who had the seven bowls came and spoke with me, saying, "Come here, I will show you the judgment of the* **great harlot** *who sits on many waters,*

The first thing we are told about the woman is that she is a whore. Why would a city be called a whore? Fornication and adultery are used in the bible in both a physical and a spiritual sense.

Example:

Isaiah 1:21, *How the faithful city has become a harlot,*

Verse 1, in Rev. 17, is using the term "whore" in its spiritual sense to identify the Catholic Church in Vatican City.

3) Rev. 17:2, *....with whom the kings of the earth committed acts of immorality, and those who dwell on the earth were made drunk with the wine of her immorality.*

Rev. 17:18, ***The woman whom you saw is the great city, which reigns over the kings of the earth.***

The Catholic Church historically appointed kings and actually reigned over them for centuries. Popes crowned and deposed kings and emperors exacting obedience by threatening them (kings) with excommunication. Though Popes lack the power to crown and depose kings today the church still retains the dogmas which authorize them to do so. The Vatican is also the only city which exchanges ambassadors with every major country on earth.

4) Rev. 17:6, *And I saw **the woman drunk with the blood of the saints**, and with the blood of the witnesses of Jesus.*

One immediately thinks of the inquisitions, Roman, Medieval, and Spanish, for centuries that was held in Europe. Spain alone the number of condemned exceeded 3 million, with about 300,000 burned at the stake. The Roman Catholic Church devised ingenious tortures that can only be described as barbaric. The remnants of some of these chambers of horror remain in Europe and may be still visited today. Protestants today have forgotten the hundreds of thousands of people burned at the stake for embracing the gospel of Christ and refusing to bow to Papal authority. Yet the Catholic Church has never officially admitted these practices were evil.

5) Rev. 17:4, *....having in her hand a **gold cup** full of abominations and of the unclean things of her immorality*

The *Catholic Encyclopedia* declares of the chalice (cup): It is the most important of sacred vessels. It may be gold or silver, and if the latter, then the inside must be surfaced with gold.

6) Rev. 17:1, ...*Come here, I will show you the judgment of the great harlot who sits on many waters,*
Rev. 17:15, *And he said to me,* "**The waters which you saw where the harlot sits, are peoples and multitudes and nations and tongues.**"
The Catholic Church is by far the largest Church on earth. Totaling 50.1% of the worlds church membership eclipsing over a billion believers. It would be much easier to list the number of countries in the world that does not have a Catholic Church than to list how many do. This church fits exactly in to verse 15's claim of a multitude of nations and tongues belonging to Catholicism.

7) Rev. 17:4, *The **woman was clothed in purple and scarlet,***
This womans colors are literally still the colors of the Catholic Clergy. The *Catholic Encyclopedia* says: A cloak the color of purple is for Bishops, for Cardinals its Scarlet.

8) Rev. 17:18, ***The woman whom you saw is the great city**, which reigns over the kings of the earth."*
The most prominent figure by far in Roman Catholicism is a woman, Mary to be exact. She over shadows all else including even God Himself. More prayers are offered to the Catholic Mary than to Christ and God combined. There are thousands of shrines to Mary around the world but scarcely more than a handful of minor shrines to Christ. In Catholicism, Christ and His sacrifice for our sins upon the cross are not enough. To be saved, the Catholic Church says one must have Marys favor, for she decides who will be in heaven.
Addressing *World Youth Day*, Pope John Paul II began: "With my heart full of praise for the queen of heaven.... This liturgy presents you, Mary, as the woman clothed with the sun.... In Mary the final

victory of life over death is already a reality.... O' Mary, as mother of the church you guide us still from your place in heaven and help us to increase in holiness by conquering sin."

It is an undeniable fact that devotion to Mary among Catholics far exceeds devotion to God or Christ. What the Catholic Church has done is turn the mother of Jesus into some sort of pagan goddess that reigns in heaven above all other entities. This Mystery Babylon meets its fate in verses 16 and 17.

Rev. 17:16, *And the ten horns which you saw, and the beast, these will hate the harlot and will make her desolate and naked, and will eat her flesh and will burn her up with fire. 17, For God has put it in their hearts to execute His purpose by having a common purpose, and by giving their kingdom to the beast, until the words of God will be fulfilled.*

Babylon #3: This Babylon listed in ch. 18, is also a prophesy, but of a future "economic Babylon" not to be confused with Mystery Babylon. Another angel informs the bible reader in verse 1 that the prophesy of Mystery Babylon is over with because of her destruction by saying "after these things" thus signaling a new prophetic message is coming.

I am going to start this section off with a deviation into the OT to the book of Zechariah. Here we will find a very strange passage that seems to apply to the Babylon prophesy in Rev. 18.

NASB5:5,
> *Then the angel who was speaking with me went out and said to me, "Lift up now your eyes and see what this is going forth." 6, I said, "What is it?" And he said, "This is the ephah going forth." Again he said, "This is their appearance in all the land 7, (and behold, a lead cover was lifted up); and this is a woman*

sitting inside the ephah." 8, *Then he said, "This is Wickedness!" And he threw her down into the middle of the ephah and cast the lead weight on its opening.* 9, *Then I lifted up my eyes and looked, and there two women were coming out with the wind in their wings; and they had wings like the wings of a stork, and they lifted up the ephah between the earth and the heavens.* 10, *I said to the angel who was speaking with me, "Where are they taking the ephah?"* 11, *Then he said to me, "To build a temple for her in the land of Shinar; and when it is prepared, she will be set there on her own **pedestal**."*

If we google nps.gov (national park service) : visiting the pedestal, we find this.

Plan Your Visit to the **Pedesta**l

Visiting the pedestal is a great addition to your trip to Liberty Island.

Sitting on top of this pedestal is none other than what Americans call the Statue of Liberty. What the prophesy in Zechariah is telling us is that at some future date a pedestal would be built for some sort of woman statute that represents evil in a land called shinar. And where is this land Shinar? The name "shi-nar" occurs 8 times in the Hebrew bible in which it refers to Babylonia. And what does Babylonia have to do with the Statue of Liberty? Why she is located just down the road from Babylon. Babylon, New York. This town was actually named after ancient Babylon and was at first called "New Babylon." Now it is just called Babylon. This third Babylon in ch. 18, of Revelations is non other than America.

1) Rev. 18:1, *She has become **a dwelling place of demons and a prison of every unclean spirit**, and a prison of every unclean and hateful bird.* I already detailed how many demonic statues and pagan names of products and companies that fill this land with demonic influence.

2) Rev. 18:2, *For **all the nations have drunk of the wine of the passion of her immorality**,* Already detailed that America is by far the #1 exporter of pornography to the world.

3) Rev. 18:11, ***And the merchants of the earth weep and mourn over her, because no one buys their cargoes any more**,* America is no longer an exporter nation but an importer nation. According to *ustr. gov*, The United States is the largest goods importer in the world.

4) Rev. 18:17, ….***And every shipmaster and every passenger and sailor, and as many as make their living by the sea**, stood at a distance,* 18, *and were crying out as they saw the smoke of her burning, saying, 'What city is like the great city?* Unlike the Babylon in Iraq which is located by a river, Babylon NY, has a deep sea port on the Atlantic ocean that ships with cargoes come in to.

5) Rev. 18:23, ….*because **all the nations were deceived by your sorcery**.* 24, *"And in her was found the blood of prophets and of saints and of all who have been slain on the earth."* Not only is America the #1 exporter of weapons to the world but we are a top exporter of the Covid 19 vaccine to the world also. *Reuters* May 20, 2021, "The United States is becoming a top supplier of COVID-19 shots to the world."

Look again at verse 23, *"deceived by your **sorcery**."* The New Testament was written in Greek. The ancient Greek word for sorcery is "pharmakeia." Today this word is known to us as pharmacy. A root word for drugs and vaccines. The next thought that should be forming in your mind is: This Covid 19 mra shot has been reported by the government VAERS system to have killed and injured over 1 million people and counting! As the fatal statistics pile up America continues to promote and administer the Covid 19 shot to all who are deceived.

This economic Babylon gets destroyed but in a different way than the other two Babylons as this one is taken out by some type of asteroid from the judgment of God.

Rev. 18:8, *For this reason in one day her plagues will come, pestilence and mourning and famine, and she will be burned up with fire; for the Lord God who judges her is strong.*

Rev. 18:21, *Then a strong angel took up a stone like a great millstone and threw it into the sea, saying, "So will Babylon, the great city, be thrown down with violence, and will not be found any longer.*

What separates this Babylon from the other two is we are told some of the Lords people are living in this economic Babylon of America and they are warned to get out.

Rev18:4, *And I heard another voice from heaven, saying, Come out of her, my people, that ye be not partakers of her sins, and that ye receive not of her plagues.*

For the rapture crowd God is telling His people it is up to them to get out. i.e. use your own feet. No angel wings or planes coming for them. So following the scriptural out of sequence list of the 3 Babylons defined in Revelations. We saw that Babylon #1 is the historic Roman empire now long gone. Babylon #2 is the Catholic Church. Only in the 3rd Babylon does God say His people must flee from making this Babylon the geographical country of America and a prophesy yet unfulfilled. .

In summary I have tried to show the reader that the elite creation of multiculturalism is the antithesis to Gods original created natural nations. That at every social, racial, and cultural level, multiculturalism causes a critical unhealthy division within the host nation it is introduced in. That it poses a dangerous threat to the security of a nation to the point of impacting that nations very survival. That multiculturalism is the precursor to globalism which will set the stage for the creation of a world governing entity called, "The New World Order." I've placed before you examples that show the American government can no longer successfully govern its own territory or its people. That Christ Himself warned us in Matthew of the disaster of a divided country. That God weighed and measured the first multicultural nation and found its existence contrary to His desires and plan for His world, thus He passed judgment on the people in Genesis 11, who were the first to come together as one. Have you acquired the understanding that my reason for writing this book is to warn the Christian body of America and of the world that there is no evidence in the bible that God ever rescinded this ancient judgment?

~ A return to the center of your culture ~

So what type of government is best? God tells us in the OT that judges are best. A group of elders tested for honesty, loyalty, and wisdom, over a life time are best to manage a people. In Acts 13, it is told that God Himself gave the people judges to rule over them.

13:20, *And after that he gave unto them judges about the space of four hundred and fifty years, until Samuel the prophet.*

Then in 1 Samuel 8, the Israelites we were told now wanted a king.

8:4, *Then all the elders of Israel gathered themselves together, and came to Samuel unto Ramah,* 5, *and said unto him, Behold, thou art old, and thy sons walk not in thy ways: now make us a king to judge us like all the nations.*

How did God feel about this? 1 Samuel 8, continues.

8:6, *But the thing displeased Samuel, when they said, Give us a king to judge us. And Samuel prayed unto the LORD.* 7, *And the LORD said unto Samuel, Hearken unto the voice of the people in all that they say unto thee: for they have not rejected thee, but they have rejected me, that I should not reign over them.*

So armed with the knowledge that democracy is not biblical in anyway and invented by Pagans for Pagans, and God Himself frowns on a king or monarchy, the bible tells us a group of judges sanctioned by God is the most suitable form of government for the Christian.
Some here may be thinking that I am advocating some kind of return to the past. That I am looking back in history and picking a time I consider to be the most ideal and want to historically turn back the clock and go back to that time. Nothing could be further from the truth. There is this thing called "First Principles." What they are is a set of undeniable truths that always will stand the test of time. A culture built on a set of first principles will stand the test of time. A few examples of first principles are:

- Two religions can never be truly equal in one country while being practiced by two racially/ethnic different people.
- Two races can never be truly equal in the same country.
- Two cultures can never be truly equal in the same country.

Why are these first principles true? Can I use Americas history to prove this point? Does not America have to force the original Christian European citizen to accept other cultures and races as equals today? Why are there Affirmative Action programs to push employers to hire minorities? Why is there an agency called the EEOC to watch dog over American businesses to protect minority employees from their employers? Why is there Fair Housing laws to force people to rent apartments and houses to minorities against their will? Why are there Civil Rights Laws to protect and promote some races but not all races?

Why are there speech codes on College Campuses to regulate the very words students may say? Why is the status of the Christian religion being lowered and removed from public view at the request of offended people with different religions today? Why does the media attack anyone they perceive as not accepting multiculturalism? Am I the only one who has figured out that if you have to force someone to recognize something as equal then it cannot be truly viewed as equal for the very reason the victim is being forced to acquire that view? Now convince me that the practicing Jew believes that the Christian religion is as good as his own. Don't tell me that the Islamic Arab believes the Christian and Jews have a religion equal to his own. Don't tell me that the Fundamentalist Christian believes all religions are equal to his own either or he would not be sending missionaries all over the world to correct the foreign non-believers minds. Don't tell me the Catholic Church does not believe they are the only true church today. The truth is there is nothing viewed as equal in any one of these world religions or even in the differing Christian religions themselves. It is an undeniable truth that if any religious person believes his church or religion is better than the rest then he already believes others outside of his church are not equal to him in one of the most personal and character defining ways.

I am calling for a return to an understanding of first principles which encompasses the true organic culture as God ordered it to be. A return to the truth. The truth is never old fashioned and never goes out of style. If a modern society cannot recognize the truth then that is a sure sign that that society is suffering from social decay and culture deterioration and will eventually by its own deeds and choices take the path to its own destructive end. A people who dwell on the fringes of their cultural realm will experience a disconnect between themselves and the very heart of their natural organic culture. It is within this far removed weakened state that the first principles that once protected and organized the people will not be present to assist them in their survival during lifes trials and adversities. For a culture to remain strong and functioning it must always be placed first and above the individual because it is the culture that defines a people. It is the culture that protects them, and it is that same culture that guides them on the path to their future. An individual is only part of it. Again Pat Buchanan said it best, "a culture is a brotherhood, you are either a part of it or you are not."

~ A Christian cannot have it both ways, therefore he must decide ~

Now for the Christian the problems our multicultural country faces today bring with it a unique set of consequential realities we should have been aware of long before this thing got so out of control. Was not America basically a Christian European nation at the beginning of its inception? What this means is Christians have dropped the ball by letting this elite created ungodly multicultural spider takeover America. When this country's courts removed Christian prayer from school the American people should have stopped working and shut this country down and marched on Washington.

So have you acquired the understanding that God was warning the world about multicultural countries by His actions in the story of the Tower of Babel? Is there any evidence that God, who tells us He is no respecter of man, changed His mind with regards to multicultural countries today? Is that same reason God separated the people in Genesis showing up in similar signs today with the elite promotion of a world governing entity some call The New World Order, and the construction of the Hadron Collider? This New World Order couldn't happen and neither could this Collider if the people of the world took Gods judgment in Genesis 11, seriously and remained racially and ethnically separate now could it?

For the Christian the issue is twofold:

1. Do you as a Christian today believe you can disregard the judgment of God in Genesis 11, that separated the people into racial nations as meaningless today?
2. Do you as a Christian believe you have the authority to reverse Gods judgment in Genesis 11, by accepting and/or promoting the reuniting of the many racial peoples of the world once again into one nation?

We as Christians will choose to learn this lesson God has given us in Genesis 11, or by our chosen actions we will set ourselves against the judgment of God.

~ 2023 ~

2016 has come and went. What we have learned is three things. One, Trump is not in the old boys club. Two, America now relies on communist Chinese voting machines for its elections. And three, the democrats can get away with stealing elections. For them to accomplish this theft this can only mean our Supreme Court is corrupt, most of our Senators and Representatives are corrupt, the FBI is corrupt, and if our Military is not corrupt then it has been proven beyond a shadow of a doubt it is useless against enemies domestic.

When the benefactor of Americas corrupt Presidential election of 2020 took office he promptly flung open our borders causing what can only be described as a full scale invasion of illegal immigrants. His assistance in this invasion includes air transport, bus trips, debit cards, cell phones, and hotel rooms. Once settled the American tax payers will be footing their other bills such as housing, ebt cards, medical care, and schooling for their young.

Since the U.S. Government has shown us in many freedom destroying ways it was so concerned about their Covid 19 plandemic spreading, what "is" their plan to keep its citizens safe from hundreds of thousands of government sponsored incoming illegal immigrants?

- *ABC10 News*, September 2021: No, migrants in immigration detention facilities are not required to get the Covid 19 vaccine.
- *Fox News*, September 9, 2021: Biden vaccination mandate doesn't include illegal immigrants.
- *New York Post*, September 20, 2021: White House defends not requiring negative Covid test from illegal immigrants.

- *Townhall* (tip sheet) September 29, 2021: House Democrats block Covid testing mandate for illegal immigrants.
- *Yahoo News*, August 12, 2021: DHS dropped 40,000 Covid 19 positive migrants in U.S. Cities says Ex. Border Chief.
- *Center for Immigration Studies*, December 10, 2021: No vaccine mandate for illegal aliens but unvaccinated Americans are blamed for spreading Covid.

And I thought the Government was serious about containing the spread of Covid? While we American citizens were losing our jobs for refusing the shot and those in our military were literally forced to get jabbed, all these hundreds of thousands of illegal immigrants were fully exempt. But if we turn our heads and look the other way we discover another group of people were also exempt from the MRA shot.

- *Newsweek*, September 10, 2021: Members of Congress and their staff are exempt from Bidens vaccine mandate.
- *Fox News*, July 23, 2021: Biden administration not mandating Covid vaccines for White House staff.

So at this point we should be asking ourselves the question: Why are only legal American citizens mandated to get this MRA shot that is not a vaccine and that was never declared to be safe for human use by the FDA because of insufficient testing?

- *VaccineImpact.com*, January 21, 2022: Over 1 million deaths and injuries following Covid Vaccinations reported by VAERS as second year of experimental use authorization begins.

VAERS is the U.S. Governments system of tracking vaccine injuries and deaths. VAERS – Vaccine Adverse Events Reporting System.

Since the U.S. Government knew these MRA shots were not properly tested for safety by the FDA they exempted themselves and all those in the medical and pharmaceutical profession from any liability that could incur from any negative reactions from patients that received "their" shot.

- **media@hhs.gov, April 14, 2023:** ....**over the past three years** the PREP Act declaration has provided liability protection for those entities engaged in manufacturing, distribution, or administration, of Covid 19 counter measures (such as tests, treatments, and vaccines).

Now that we are well into 2023 and the Governments own VAERS tracking system has documented over 1 million MRA shot injuries and deaths, the Covid 19 shot has been halted right?

- *6News, Richmond,* June 21, 2023: Next round of Covid 19 shots in fall will target latest Omicron Strain.
- *Reuters*, June 12, 2023: Covid shots should target XRB variants in 2023 – 2024 campaign U.S. FDA staff say.
- *Verywell Health*, February 15, 2023: Moderna Covid vaccines will be free in 2023.

In the interest of Public Safety what precautions has your Government taken in their ongoing fight against Covid?

- **media@hhs.gov, April 14, 2023:** (con't) the PREP Act immunity from liability **will be extended through 2024** for those entities engaged in manufacturing, distribution, or administration, of Covid 19 counter measures (such as tests, treatments, and vaccines).

It is now 2023 and for those concerned this is what we know now.

- Covid 19 was proven to be at least 97.9% survivable.

- Known cures such as Hydroxychloroquine and Ivermectin were suppressed by the U.S. Government and by many in the medical profession.
- This coordinated suppression of known cures allowed the Government to declare an emergency during the Covid plandemic which gave them two things. One, the power to force an untested MRA shot on American citizens. And Two, it sanctioned the Emergency Use Authorization (EUA) which created an umbrella of immunity for all involved in its creation and administration.
- VAERS, the government tracking system for vaccine negative events recorded over 1 million deaths and injuries *and still counting*, caused by their Covid 19 shot
- The Government exempted themselves and all illegal aliens from getting their MRA shot.

At this point in time the word that should be forming on the lips of the legal American citizen is "replacements."

www.ingramcontent.com/pod-product-compliance
Lightning Source LLC
Chambersburg PA
CBHW061258110426
42742CB00012BA/1971